THE POLITICAL ECONOMY OF THE STATE IN INDIA

ASHUTOSH KUMAR

ATLANTIC PUBLISHERS & DISTRIBUTORS

Published by
ATLANTIC PUBLISHERS & DISTRIBUTORS
B-2, Vishal Enclave, New Delhi-110027
Phone: 5413460

Sales office
4346/4C, Ansari Road, Darya Ganj,
New Delhi-110002
Phone: 3273880

Typeset at
APD COMPUTER GRAPHICS
B-2, Vishal Enclave, New Delhi-110027

Printed in India at
Mehra Offset Press
New Delhi

Acknowledgements

First thanks goes to my students at Jammu University who convinced me of the need for a survey analysis of Marxist and Neo-marxist literature concerning the class character of the state in the post-colonial societies in general and Indian society in particular and contributed in their own way by their sincere involvement in the class discussions and seminars.

I owe a great debt of gratitude to my former teachers and friends for being constant source of inspiration and support in my all past and present academic endeavours. A complete listing would be impossible but at the very least. it would include: Prof. Randhir Singh, Prof. Manoranjan Mohanty, Prof. M.P. Singh, Prof. R.B. Jain and Dr. B.B. Sarkar of the Department of Political Science, Delhli University an my friends Deepak Verma, Manindra Thakur, Satish Jha, Mani Bhushan, all teaching in the different colleges of Delhi University. For specific comments and criticisms of some of the chapters I am indebted to Dr. Neera Chandhoke, who as my teacher and guide, has always taken keen interest in my academic pursuits. But the greatest debt of gratitude I owe to Ujjwal Singh of the Department of Political Science, Hindu College, with whom I have shared most fruitful intellectual collaboration in the exciting field of research on State theory.

Ashutosh Kumar

Acknowledgements

[illegible]

[illegible]

PREFACE

The Book raises two Pertinent questions. The First one is as to why we need to study the state and Secondly, why do we need to study the state in the post-colonial Indian society in particular.

The increasing importance of the state has to be reiterated. The increasing visibility of the state in every day life has been paralleled by increasingly sophisticated and complex intellectual theorizing on the nature of state. In fact, there is no sphere in our life which has remained unaffected by the state.

Scholars belonging to diverse theoretical predilections from all the main disciplines have attempted to highlight the state as an actor in the political arena in his own light. The rank of the topics explored in relation to the state has been very wide. The scholars of Latin America, Africa and Asia have, in particular, examined the roles of post-colonial states in instituting comprehensive political reforms, helping to shape national economic development, and bargaining with multinational corporations, on the other hand social scientists interested in the advanced industrial societies have probed the involvements of state in developing social programs and in managing domestic and international economic problems.

In the second place, I have chosen to probe the nature of the state in the post-colonial societies. Here it must be emphasized that though the importance of state in the advanced societies is growing, the growth in the sphere of post-colonial states activity has been far more phenomenal. Thus, there is now hardly any aspect of social, economic and cultural life which is untouched by the post-colonial state. In fact, decolonization has resulted in notably top heavy states even comparable in its sway to the colonial state. The rapid growth of state in the post-colonial societies has motivated many scholars to look into the nature of the state. Recently a lot of theorization has taken place upon the nature of the post-colonial state both within the liberal as well as the Marxist Paradigms. The same remains true with regard to the nature of state in post-colonial Indian society. In the survey of literature on the nature of the state in the book, primarily the views of those political scientists have been taken into consideration whose predilections are essentially

Marxists. According to Paul Baran Marxism is and must be treated as 'an intellectual attitude or a way of thought, a philosophical position the fundamental principle of which is continuous, systematic and comprehensive confrontation of reality with reason'.

As we would see while dealing with the Marxist theory of the state, no other aspect of Marxian thought has been so greatly blurred as the theory of state because Marx himself did not attempt to set out a comprehensive and systematic theorization of state. Marx had given the outline of a theory of state. Subsequently, this theory has been elaborated by the Marxists taking the 'fundamentals' in due consideration. This is true not only for the theorization on the advanced capitalist state but also on the post-colonial state in general and Indian state in particular.

Though within the liberal paradigm, a great number of works have come up analyzing political regimes in terms of development or modernization, they have ignored not only the state but also the domination-dependence relationship which constitute the history of these post-colonial societies. In fact, these theories have raised more questions than answered them. Their analyses lack the comprehension of the material base, class contradiction or class struggle. The analyses of the liberal theorists have remained a historical, static, status-quoist and ethno-centric. They tend to ignore the dislocations caused by colonialism, the dialectical inter-twining of the colonial experience with the pre-colonial one.

Thus to avoid the theoretical pitfalls of the liberal theorists, logic leads us to a Marxist approach which views society as the outcome of historical forces looking various dimensions of society in a meaningful manner. Its level of analysis includes substructure as well as superstructure, the methodology's materialist as well as historical and social conflict as well as cooperation is incorporated. Moreover it grounds its theorization in the material base, and locates class struggle as the fundamental dynamic.

In the recent upsurge concerning the theorization on the post-colonial state in general and Indian state in particular, we have been witnessing a viewpoint which has come to be known as Neo-Marxist. The Neo-Marxists grapple with the social-economy problems and historical specificities of the post-colonial societies and thus have modified the Marxist position sufficiently. The Neo-Marxism represents a trend within the Marxist tradition, and have contributed in developing the tenets of Marxist thought in the historical context of post-colonial societies.

In fact, all Marxists or Neo-Marxists agree that they have to come to grips with the nature and function of the state if they wish to understand the bases of the Policy-making process. They recognise the fundamental role of state in political and economic activity.

There is a problem which the Marxist political scientists face invariably whether they are 'Orthodox Marxists' or 'Neo-Marxists'. In fact what has so far been said about the Marxist view of the state mainly referred to its nature and role in advanced capitalist societies. So automatically it has not been possible to transpose simply the categories of analysis used for the state in the advanced capitalist societies to these different economic, social and political structures. The problem that they face is the manner in which these categories have to be applied to post-colonial societies. In fact the post-colonial states are placed in a specific time and specific . Dependency, weak social structure, classes-information are the factors which distinguish these states. Due to the colonization as well as external capitalist domination the development of these post-colonial states in general and Indian state in particular have been distorted which can be seen in their economic, social and political structures.

In the face of these factors, Marxists have a formidable task in comprehending the complex nature of the post-colonial societies. The debates on the nature of post-colonial societies and the 'specificity of the Political' in these societies are based on the certain fundamentals in Marxist theory. The book examines these fundamentals also. A theoretical survey of the view of the mainstream communist parties on the nature of the post-colonial Indian state has been also undertaken in the course of the work as despite their ideological rigidity their's views remain complementary to theoretical debate with regard to nature of Indian state.

Ashutosh Kumar

Contents

CHAPTER I

THE STATE AND MARXIAN THEORY

The theory of the state is the core of Marxian thought and, as has been the case with many other Marxian theories and concepts, the Marxian theory of State has been focal point of the debate in the Marxist academic circles. Wide ranging controversies have raged around this theory. In the recent years, the debate has become much more intensified. As a matter of fact no other aspect of Marxism has been so greatly blurred, distorted and befogged[1] as this. This has happened largely due to the fact that Marx and Engels never attempted to formulate a comprehensive and systematic theory of State.

In the absence of a complete and coherent account of the state by Marx and Engels their views on the subject have been studied mainly through the later interpretations of their works. These different, often conflicting, interpretations have been affected both by changing political circumstances and by piecemeal discovery and publication of some of Marx's manuscripts, which have raised new questions about the development of his thought. These interpretations and adaptations fail to constitute an adequate expression of Marx's own views, also because they emphasise some aspects of his thought to the detriment of others, and thus distort by over-simplification an extremely complex and by no means unambiguous body of ideas. They also completely neglect certain strands in Marx's thought which are of considerable interest and importance.[2]

With reference to above, it is imperative to analyse what Marx himself, than any of his interpretors, has actually theorized about the nature of state. Pertinently there is lot more on the state in Marxian thought than has been generally accepted. An outline of Marx's overall project gives the state a much more important role in his explanation of capitalism than would appear to be the case from a glance at his finished work. For instance 'Capital', Marx's great work, contains a theory of state which, unlike Marx's related economic theories, has never been fully worked out.[3] In fact his first lengthy piece of writing after his doctoral dissertation, namely 'Critique of the Hegelian Philosophy of Right', is to a large extent concerned with the analysis of the state. The subject also receives extended treatment in Marx's historical writings as 'The Class Struggle in France", 'The Eighteenth Brumaire of Louis Bonaparte' and 'The Civil War in France'. His ideas on the nature of State also emanate from his journalistic works as well as incidental remarks he made about state. In addition, Engels, too, dealt at length with the state in 'Anti-Duhring' and also in 'The Origin of the Family, Private Property and the State', his last work.

Very naturally, these different works have led to a variety of interpretations especially in the recent years. However, despite the differences in the interpretations, all Marxist writers, in one form or another, do derive their state 'theories' from some Marxist 'fundamentals', and it is these analytical fundamentals that frame the recent Marxist debate about the theory of state.[4] In the present paper an attempt would be made to deal with the analytical fundamentals.

As mentioned above, Marx's engagement with the theoretical issues related to state developed from an early encounter with Hegel. Marx, himself, has traced his development of the concept of state back to his critique of Hegelian concept of state and society. Marx said in 'Contribution to the Critique of Political Economy' that his investigation led to the result that legal relations as well as forms of the state are to be grasped neither from themselves nor from the so-called general development of the human mind, but rather have their roots in the material conditions of life, the sum total of which Hegel, following the example of the Englishmen and the Frenchmen of the Eighteenth century, combines under the name of 'Civil Society', that however, the 'antatomy of civil society is to be sought in the political economy'. Marx goes on to say, "In the social production of their life, men enter into definite relations that are indispensable and independent of their will, relations of production which correspond to a sum total of these relations of production constitute the economic structure of a society, the real foundation, on which rises a legal and political superstructure and to which corresponds definite forms of social consciousness. The mode of production of material life conditions the social, political and intellectual life process in general."[5] This formulation of the state views the economic structure as the basis of the social and political structures. The form of the state, therefore, emanates from the relations of production and not from the general development of the human mind or from the collective of men's wills. Unlike Hegel, Marx places State into a historical context and makes it a subject to the materialist conception of history. For Marx, it is the civil society that shapes the state. This position is diametrically opposed to Hegel who contends that it is the state that shapes the society.

In 'The Philosophy of Right', Hegel argued that state is an embodiment of society's general interest and that it remains over and above the particular interests. Thus state can be able to overcome the division between civil society and itself as well as the split between the individual as a private person and citizen. But this, says Marx, is simply not true. The contradiction between the State and the society is real enough. Rejecting the Hegelian view of the state as a trustee of the society, Marx says that state, in all the cases, remains subordinate to capital. Far from being above class struggles, state, therefore, becomes the political expression of the dominance of the bourgeoisie in a capitalist society, 'There may be occasions and matters where the interest of all classes happen to coincide. But for the most part and in essence, these interests are fundamentally and irrevocably at odds, so that the state cannot possibly be their common trustee, the idea that it can is part of the ideological veil which a dominant class draws upon the reality of class rule, so as to legitimate that rule in its own eyes as well as in the eyes of the subordinate classes.'[6] In the 'Critique to the Hegel's Philosophy of Right' Marx advocated the achievement of democracy as a measure to enable state to defend general interest. However, Marx soon moved on to the view that the achievement of democracy and the resultant 'Political emancipation' was incapable of bringing about a 'human emancipation.'[7] This objective, according to Marx, required a much more thorough reorganization of society,[8] of which the main feature was the abolition of private property.

The view of the state as the instrument of an economically and therefore politically dominant bourgeoisie remained fundamental to the Writings of Marx and Engels. Engels, for instance, said in 'The Origin of the Family, Private Property and the State', "State arose from the need to hold class antagonisms in check, but because it arose, at the same time, in the midst of the conflicts of these classes, it is, as a rule, the state of the most powerful, economically dominant class, which, through the medium of the state, becomes also the politically dominant class, and thus acquires new means of holding down and exploiting the oppressed class. Thus the state of antiquity was above all the state of the slave owners for the purpose of holding down the slaves, as the feudal state was the organ of the nobility for holding down the peasants, serfs and bondsmen and the modern representative state is an instrument of exploitation of wage labour by capital."[9] This formulation, however, does not touch upon the basic question as to why and how the state, as an institution separate from the ruling class, plays this role. The question becomes specifically pertinent in the context of the bourgeois society, where the distance between the state and economic forces is generally quite marked.[10]

In the recent years, two different approaches have been used to provide an answer to the above-mentioned question.[11] The first approach hinges on the numerous ideological and political factors: for instance, the pressures brought on the state by bourgeoisie and also the ideological congruence between the bourgeoisie and the state bureaucracy. Thus the top personnel of the bourgeois state system "have tended to belong to the same class or classes which have dominated the other strategic heights of the society, notably the economic and cultural ones. Thus in contemporary capitalism, members of the bourgeoisie tend to predominate in the three main sectors of social life, the economic, the political and the cultural/ideological."[12] Added to this is the enormous economic power of the bourgeoisie due to its ownership and control of economic resources which enables the bourgeoisie to bring decisive influence over the state and its bureaucracy.

The second approach which Marxists have used to provide an answer the question as to why the state should be thought to be an 'instrument' of a capitalist 'ruling class', emphasizes the 'structural constraints' to which the state is subjected in a capitalist society. The basic argument is that the state cannot be anything but an 'instrument' of the bourgeoisie because, 'given its insertion in the capitalist mode of production it cannot be anything else.'[13] Thus those who run the state apparatus recognise and subscribe to the logic of 'structural imperative' of capitalism, which imposes itself at each step, as well as in the long run, upon the making of public policy. There may be miscalculations and temporary disjunctions between the objective needs of capitalism and state policies. But, in the final analysis, the demands of capitalism impose themselves upon the state as inexorable necessity. As Miliband puts it, "A capitalist economy has its own 'rationality' to which any Government and state must sooner or later submit, and usually sooner."[14]

Notwithstanding the differences between them, both approaches treat state as subservient to and constrained by the forces and the pressures external to itself, capitalists in the first and capital in the second. However this conceptualization of the capitalist state as an instrument leaves out of account a significant part of the view of state in Marxist Thought. For Marx and Engels attributed to the state relative autonomy from the capitalist 'ruling class' and from civil society at large. This notion of the 'relatively autonomous' state constitute a major part of the Marxist theory of the state and was widely discussed by Marx and Engels in their historical writings. Hal Draper contends that this conceptualization of state with considerable autonomy threads its way into the later class analysis of the state. He states, "Marx and Engels did not make the state out to be merely an extrusion of the ruling class, its tool, puppet, or reflection in some simplistic, passive sense ... Rather the state arises from and expresses a real overall need for the organization of society – a need which exists no matter what is the particular class structure. But as long as there is a ruling class in socio-economic relations, it will utilize this need to shape and control the state along its own class lines.'[15] The conceptualization concedes a certain amount of autonomy to the state even under the normal conditions.

Under 'abnormal conditions', Marx and Engels attribute to state a far greater amount of autonomy. This is common a view in the historical studies of different forms of state embedded not only in different modes of production and social formations, but also in the capitalist mode of production itself. These different forms of state ranging from 'Asiatic' despotism to the Absolutist state, and including the states of Antiquity and of feudalism. Based on the concrete studies Marx and Engels also distinguished between such forms of state as the bourgeois republic, the Bonapartist and Bismarckian states, the English and Czarist forms of state.

In his study of 'The Eighteenth Brumaire of Louis Bonaparte', Marx refers to the French state as "(his) executive power, with its enormous bureaucratic and military organization, with its ingenious state machinery, embracing wide strata, with a host of officials numbering half a million, besides an army of another half million, this appalling parasitic body which enmeshes the body of French society like a net and choken all its pores, sprang up in the days of the absolute monarchy with the decay of the feudal system which it helped to hasten. The seigniorial privileges of the landowners and towns were transformed into so many attributes of the state power, the feudal dignitaries into paid officials, and the motely pattern of conflicting medieval plenary powers into the regulated plan of a state authority whose works is divided and centralized as in a factory." Marx goes on to say, "Every common interest was straightway severed from society, counterpoised to it as a higher, general interest, snatched from the activity of society's members themselves and made an object of Government activity."[16] Thus France, according to Marx seemed to escape the "despotism of an individual and, what is more, beneath the authority of an individual without authority. The struggle seems to be settled in such a way that all classes, equally impotent and equally mute, fall on their knees before the rifle butt."[17] The Bonapartist state armed with enormous executive power made itself completely independent of civil society.

In the same vein, Marx refers to the Prussian state as "a state which is no more than a military despotism and a police state, bureaucratically carpentered, embellished with parliamentary forms and disguised by an admixture of feudalism."[18] Similar ostensive definitions are offered by Engels in his historical studies of England, Germany and other countries.

Engels, for instance, in his last work, 'The Origin of the Family, Private Property and the State' characterizes both the Bonapartist and Bismarckian states as the states enjoying a very high degree of independence, albeit 'by way of exception'. He states, "By way of exception, however, periods occur in which the warring classes balance each other so nearly that the state power, as ostensible mediator, acquires, for the moment, a certain degree of independence of both. Such was the absolute monarchy of the seventeenth and eighteenth centuries, which held the balance between the nobility and the class of burghers, such was the Bonapartism of the first and still more of the second French Empire, which played off the proletariat against the bourgeoisie and the bourgeoisie against the proletariat. The latest performance of this kind ... is the new German Empire of the Bismarck nation: here capitalists and workers are balanced against each other and equally cheated for the benefit of the impoverished Prussian Cabbage Junkers."[19]

Pertinently, the relative autonomy of the state was primarily acknowledged by Marx and Engels in relation with forms of state where the executive power dominated all other elements of the state system. The absolutist state, the Bonapartist or Bismarckian one are such instances. The autonomy of these states is far more considerable as the executive power is least constrained either by other elements within the state system, or by various forces in the civil society.

These formulations appear to be suggesting not only that the state enjoys a 'relative autonomy', but that it has made itself completely independent of all social forces in civil society. This concept depart radically from the classical notion of state as a class state. However, it's not the case as Marx goes on to say in the context of the Bonapartist state, that "The state power does not hang in mid-air" and that Bonaparte did represent a class, indeed he represents the most numerous class of French society, the small-holding peasants."[20] This happened at a time "when the bourgeoisie had already lost, and the working class had not yet acquired, the faculty of ruling the nation."[21] Marx wrote that the Bourgeoisie, in particular "confesses that its own interests dictate that it should be delivered from the danger of its rule, that in order to restore tranquility in the country, its bourgeois parliament must, first of all, be given its quietus: that in order to preserve its social power in fact, its political power must be broken."[22] In this situation, 'Imperialism', Marx states, here meaning the Bonapartist regime, "Is, at the same time, the most prostitute, and the ultimate form of the state power which nascent middle class society had commenced to elaborate as a means of its own emancipation from feudalism, and which full-grown bourgeois society had finally transformed into a means for the enslavement of labour by capital."[23] Thus the Bonapartist state served the capitalist system by serving the economic interests of the bourgeoisie. This it did by not changing the capitalist relations of production and thereby leaving the basic control over the economy in the hands of the capitalists. Marx thus describes Bonaparte as "the executive authority which has attained power in its own right, and as such he feels it to be his mission to safeguard 'bourgeois order'."[24] Thus Bonapartist state has a class base and the class function. On the other hand, the notion of the state as serving to perpetuate a certain 'equilibrium' between 'warring classes' emerges in the observation of Marx and Engels on the subject of absolutism.[25] This formulation was also used by Engels to describe both the Bonapartist state and the Bismarckian state.

Nevertheless, the relative autonomy of the state, even if it is of high order, does not reduce its class character: on the contrary, its relative independence makes it possible for the state to play its class role in an appropriately flexible manner. If it really was the simple 'instrument' of the 'ruling class', it would be fatally inhibited in the performance of its role. Its agents absolutely need a measure of freedom in deciding how best to serve the existing social order.[26] Thus the relatively autonomous capitalist state is in a better position to constantly act or intervene, apparently against the bourgeoisie but really in its behalf, to alleviate the anarchy of the market, to prevent major depression, or to save capitalism from its self-destructive consequences. The course followed by capitalist state is also influenced, within limits set by the basic need of preserving as well as reproducing the capitalist order, by other factors like conflicts between long run and short run interests of the ruling class, between the interests of the bourgeoisie as a whole and of its particular sections or between particular interests of its different sections. In this context Marx and Engels said in 'The Communist Manifesto', "The executive of the modern state is but a committee for managing the common affairs of the whole bourgeoisie."[27] Thus while each capitalist can manage his particular interest, only state armed with relative autonomy can manage the 'common' affairs of the 'whole' capitalist class and this is a profoundly different kind of management altogether.

Thus the Marxian theory of state has nothing to do with the vulgar notion often attributed to Marx and Engels – as for example by Deane, when he speaks of 'the simple and monolithic Marxist analysis of the state' – that the state always and everywhere and automatically, in a simple and predetermined manner, serves the 'sole purpose of defending the interests of the ruling class.'[28] Interpretations of this type are misleading and deserve to be rejected. In this context Miliband spell out the basic elements in a Marxist account of the state in the following words, "While the state does act, in Marxist terms, on behalf of the 'ruling class', it does not for the most part act at its behest." State, despite being a class state, "enjoys a high degree of autonomy and independence in the manner of its operation as class state and indeed must have that high degree of autonomy and independence if it is to act as a class state."[29]

References

1. Henry Lefebvre, 'The Sociology of Marx', London, Allen Lan The Penguin Press, 1968, p. 123.
2. Ralph Miliband, 'Marx and the State' in Ralph Miliband and John Saville (eds.), 'The Socialist Register', London, The Merlin Press Ltd., 1965, p. 278.
3. Simon Clarke opines, "The State is not a hidden presupposition of capital, it is a concept that has to be developed on the basis of the analysis offered in capital", Simon Clarke, 'State, class struggle and capitalist reproduction', Berkeley, Kapilistat, No. 10-11.
4. Martin Carnoy, 'The State and Political Theory', Princeton, New Jersey, Princeton University Press, 1984, p. 46.

5. K. Marx, "Contribution to the Critique of Political Economy", in Marx and Engels, 'Selected Works', Vol. I, Moscow, Progress Publishers, 1969-70, p. 503.
6. Ralph Miliband, 'Marxism and Politics', Oxford, Oxford University Press, p. 66.
7. Ralph Miliband, 'The State', in Tom Bottomore edited, 'A Dictionary of Marxist Thought', Oxford, Blackwell Reference, 1983, p. 465.
8. Anthony Giddens, 'Capitalism and Modern Social Theory', Cambridge, Cambridge University Press, 1990, p. 6.
9. Friedrich Engels, 'The Origin of the Family, Private Property and the State' in Marx and Engels, 'Selected Works', Vol. 3, Moscow, Progress Publishers, 1969-70, p. 332.
10. Ralph Miliband, N. 7, p. 465.
11. Roger King, 'The State in Modern Society', London, Macmillan, 1979, p. 63.
12. Ralph Miliband, N. 6, p. 68-69.
13. *Ibid.*, p. 72.
14. *Ibid.*
15. Hal Draper, 'Karl Marx's Theory of Revolution', State and Bureaucracy', Vol. I, New York, Monthly Review Press, 1977, p. 319.
16. Karl Marx, 'Surveys from, Exile', in 'Political Writings', Vol. II, London, Pelican, 1973, p. 237-238.
17. *Ibid.*, p. 236.
18. Karl Marx, 'Critique of the Gotha Programme', quoted in Bob Jessop, 'The Capitalist State', Oxford, Martin Robertson, 1982, p. 21.
19. F. Engels, N. 9, pp. 328-29.
20. Karl Marx, N. 16, p. 238.
21. Karl Marx, 'The First International and After', in 'Political Writings', Vol. 3, London, Pelican, p. 208.
22. Karl Marx and Friedrich Engels, 'Collected Works', London, Lawrence and Wishart, 1979, p. 143.
23. Karl Marx, N. 21, p. 208.
24. Karl Marx, N. 16, p. 245.
25. Refer: Perry Anderson, 'Lineages of the Absolutist State', London, New Left Books, 1974.
26. Ralph Miliband, N. 6, p. 87.
27. K. Marx and F. Engels, 'The Communist Manifesto' in Marx and Engels, 'Selected Works', Vol. I, Moscow, Progress, 1969-70, p. 110.
28. Herbert A. Deane, 'The Political Ideas of Harold J. Laski', New York, 1955, pp. 153-69.
29. Ralph Miliband, N. 6, p. 74.

CHAPTER II

CLASS AND STATE IN THE POST-COLONIAL SOCIETIES

Theories on the relation of class and state in the post-colonial societies have approached the subject from varying perspectives and with reference to differing specific questions. These include the questions of whether a ruling class can be identified and, if so, the nature of its composition, the class nature of the State, and the specific relation of indigenous to foreign capital and of each to the state. These interconnected issues have been treated in different manners by different theorists partly because the theorists have focused on differing specific cases, but also because of reliance on varying underlying assumptions and, at times, on less than complete or coherent theoretical frameworks.

In general, however, the various interpretations may be summarized as coinciding with one of several positions. One is that the state is just an instrument of capital, either metropolitan or indigenous, or a combination of these. In contrast to this is the view that the class nature of the state remains undetermined and that no ruling class can be identified. Between these two positions are further formulations which stress the importance of state personnel, not merely as implementer of policy but as fundamentally responsible for state orientation and developmental direction. On the one hand, the alliance of sections of the capitalist class is extended to include a new element, *i.e.* the bureaucratic or state bourgeoisie. This element has been frequently regarded as having a dominant position within a ruling alliance; on occasion it is characterized as constituting a dominant or ruling class in its own right, the autonomy of the state from capital thereby being manifest in the emergence of a distinct independent class. On the other hand, state personnel are included as an element in an entirely new indigenous class conceived of as straddling state and civil society and incorporating indigenous capitalists and sometimes professionals as well as high level state and party personnel.

The variety of models and the proliferation of new constructs reflect attempts to come grips with the apparently unique features of the post-colonial society. The development of the post-colonial societies has been exceedingly distorted by colonialism and external capitalist domination, which is manifest in their economic, social and political structures.[1] Thus the categories of analysis used for the advanced capitalist societies cannot be simply transposed to the post-colonial societies. To quote Miliband "Marxism, primarily fashioned in and for a bourgeois/ capitalist context has, to say the least, to be adapted to the very different circumstances."[2] One should also bear in mind variable effect of historical and socio-economic considerations upon the post-colonial societies which makes it difficult to attempt to formulate generalization with any degree of certainty while analyzing class character of the post-colonial states. Thus differences related to the nature of precapitalist social formations, mode of capitalist intervention and experience of colonization make the application of generalizations problematic as the level of analysis approaches the concrete. However the common relation of the post-colonial societies to imperialism does permit some degree of generalization. Conceptualization of the state and its class nature have been generalized to all cases within the periphery.

The State as an Instrument of Capital

The general understanding following from an instrumentalist Marxist analysis is that the bourgeoisie is the determinant influence on capitalist states. It may not rule directly either by supplying personnel to the state or directing the activities of a governing party. But its position in the economy is such that it manifests 'latent' political power; reproduction of the economy implies reproduction of bourgeoisies dominant position *vis-a-vis* other indigenous classes, and the policy of a state whose fundamental object is societal reproduction necessarily reflects this dominance.

To the extent that the post-colonial state is regarded as capitalist or with the capitalist mode of production gaining ascendancy and assuming relative dominance within the economy, it remains an instrument of capital. Many Neo-Marxist works on the post-colonial state have affirmed the critical importance of capital in determining, constraining, or limiting the scope of policy which can be effectively implemented.[3] However in contrast to western capitalism, where the interests of a national bourgeoisie enjoy primacy, the dominant segment of bourgeoisie in the post-colonial states is generally externally based. Accordingly Metropolitan bourgeoisie is frequently regarded as exerting the decisive influence on the post-colonial state.

With reference to the above, the notion of 'neo-colonialism' was advanced to argue that political independence brought little change to the economy and therefore the indirect political dominance of imperial capital continued. The post-colony was simply a new form, political 'freedom' for the indigenous population merely a new cloak, under which the basic mechanism of reproduction sustained imperialist hegemony. The dependency theorists tend to affirm this point of view and generalize it to all post-colonial economics. The very term depending highlighted assumed mechanism for continued subordination. The dependent economy could not be reproduced except as an adjunct of world imperialism. The peripheral state was a dependent political apparatus. It's personnel formulated policies which necessarily coincided with the long term interests of the metropole. It's local political base, when identified as indigenous capital, was regarded as a comprador class, a client group, an auxiliary bourgeoisie. Consequently the post-colonial state may be strong and autonomous *vis-a-vis* it's local bourgeosie, but it remains largely an instrument of the imperialist bourgeoisie of the metropolis.[4]

In reaction to the bourgeois modernization models, the Neo-Marxist dependency school tended to emphasise and perhaps overemphasise the decisiveness of metropolitan control and thus to de-emphasise local class processes and their independent effects on the post-colonial state.[5] With their overemphasis on unequal exchange relations between a core and a periphery, social classes became synonymous with geographical entities and problems of inequality and deprivation thus making the prospect of any meaningful class analysis of the post-colonial state extremely unlikely.[6]

In due course the dependency theory's hypothesis was subjected to criticism. For a many Neo-Marxists, independence did constitute a significant change in power relations and made possible the diversion of policy away from the immediate interests of metropolitan capital. State capitalism, especially where involving expropriation or partial take over of metropolitan property, has been viewed as an expression of this change, as a national, anti-imperialist strategy taken up when the indigenous bourgeoisie is incapable of displacing metropolitan capital.

Even when metropolitan capital was assumed to retain economic dominance, dependence regarded some coverage as falling to the indigenous classes – so that within limits placed by the overwhelming presence of metropolitan capital on the 'free choice' of policy, the actions of the state were regarded as subject to local class pressures.[7]

Concern with the impact of local class formation on the State has motivated numerous analysis of the growth of indigenous capital. Even where seen as 'weak', indigenous capitalist class is frequently considered to have discernible political impact. For Patankar and Omvedt, it is the local bourgeoisie which holds state power in most post-colonial societies.[8] Thus some theorists place indigenous bourgeoisie in alliance with metropolitan capital in constituting a dominant class but who posit that the indigenous bourgeoisie may qualify in its own right as a ruling class.

While conceding that indigenous Kenyan capital does not act independently of the international capitalist system and that its development is therefore hardly autonomous, Swainson strenously rejects the view that its base is in large scale capitalist production. She regards it as clearly an 'important political element' and not merely as an 'adjunct to the dominant foreign capital.'[9]

Colin Leys takes up Swainson's argument and develops it further. Doing a concrete study of Kenya, Leys refutes the view of the state as an independent mediator between foreign and local capital, with metropolitan bourgeoisie being the stronger and local bourgeoisie making only minor gains. Leys regards the post-colonial state as collaborating with the indigenous bourgeoisie in assault on barriers inherited from colonialism that constrain advancement in technology.[10]

With reference to above Beckman has emphasised the need for caution in the discussion and argued for avoidance of too great a preoccupation with the question of whether the state is more clearly the instrument of indigenous as opposed to metropolitan capital. What must not be lost in assessment of the conflict of interests and the relative moulding of policy toward one or the other is the point alluded to by Colin Leys: that there is an overarching unity of capital and that the state is ultimately subjected to the logic of capital in general.[11]

In all cases, whether seen as the instrument of bourgeoisie in general or more narrowly of metropolitan or indigenous bourgeoisie, those who regard the post-colonial state as capitalist in nature affirm that the interests of capital dictate its developmental direction. In a class differentiated society with economically dominant and subordinate classes the state remains "an integral element of the overall structure of society with the function of upholding and maintaining the class based social order and relations of class domination and subordination."[12] There may be temporary disjunctions between the objective needs of peripheral capitalism and state policies. But in the final analysis "the demands of peripheral capitalism impose themselves upon the post-colonial state as inexorable necessity."[13]

Class Nature of the State Undetermined

In spite of its clear expression since the end of colonialism, indigenous bourgeoisies in the post-colonial states have often been described as Weak.[14] Its weakness is registered in the small size of individual enterprises, its command over only a small proportion of economic activity, and its concentration in commerce and virtual exclusion from productive enterprise. Its proportionate share of economic control generally remains far below that of metropolitan bourgeoisie. Thus decolonization is seen as involving the creation of a state very different from those of the west, characterized by sinking discontinuity between economic control and the direct exercised political power. No local propertied class is sufficiently strong to assume political prominence even indirectly or behind the scenes. And the fact of independence precludes the economically dominant, metropolitan capital, from occupying the role of ruling class.

Not only is indigenous bourgeoisie considered weak but the process of class formation itself is often regarded as still in its initial state, with the post-colonial societies engaged in a transition from a combined mode (*i.e.* feudal and capitalist modes) to one which a single capitalist mode of production becomes generalized. As Claude Ake puts it, "so say the class contradictions have not matured owing to its embryonic industrial structure."[15] For instance the work-force has not completely severed its ties with the peasantry and thus remains less than a full-fledged proletariat. There is also a high incidence of straddling class positions, a high rate of individual mobility through class locations and a high proportion of the population simultaneously involved in both capitalist and non-capitalist production relations (*e.g.* relations based on kinship ties). Thus the coherence of class forces may be limited,[16] all the more so given the nature of the independence struggle which entained an alliance of different classes around the issue of political nationalism.

In the same vein, Szentes even after acknowledging the existence of certain class groups, sees the class structure as undefined. Neither local capital nor any other class, he suggests, is able to exert decisive influence over state activity. Regarding the state as therefore less tied to existing class forces in an underdeveloped than in a developed social formation, Szentes suggests that it is possible that the state might outgrow its initial functions of undermining the precapitalist elements and of fastening the process of accumulation through direct intervention. In the process it's very behaviour in setting limits to the growth of private capital might establish the basis for an "overture to socialist development without a socialist revolutionary transformation."[17] This characterization of the transitional nature of the class structure leads Stains *et. al.* to view the post-colonial state as having an important independent role and to posit the possibility of its personnel opting for non-capitalist as opposed to capitalist development.

The notion that classes remain incompletely formed in the post-colonial states, with no single class capable of exerting decisive influence over the state, underlies a number of works. For instance to quote Ian Roxborough: "The class structures of the Third World differ from those of the advanced nations in two principle ways – they are more complex, and the classes themselves are usually much weaker. Not only the class structures of the underdeveloped nations complex and weak, they are also incomplete in the sense that the dominant class is absent."[18]

State Personnel as Constituting a Dominant Class

In the context of weak or indeterminate or incomplete class formations in the post-colonial states, John Saul argues that the nature of politics and of state personnel become decisive in the formulation of state policies. Given the apparent inability of indigenous capital to constitute a dominant class bureaucracy emerges as a dominant class. According to Saul, due to weak character of indigenous bourgeoisie, it find itself enmeshed in bureaucratic controls by which "those at the top of the hierarchy of the bureaucratic military apparatus of the state are able to maintain and even extend their dominant power in society."[19] Similarly Hamza Alavi, states that in the post-colonial states, "those at the top of the hierarchy of the bureaucratic military apparatus of the state are able to maintain and even extend their dominant power in society."[20] This happens because those personnel who occupy the leading positions in the state systems use "their power, *inter alia*, to advance their own economic interests, and the economic interests of their families, friends and followers, or clients."[21]

Thus while Saul refers to transitory and unformed status of those in the political apparatus, Miliband in contrast focuses on their potential for recognition of self interest. However both Neo-Marxists imply that the nature of policy is to be largely understood by examination of those in positions of power with attention to their class background and their potential interests.

In more general terms, Ziemann and Lanzendorfer have argued that the central role of the state in the peripheral society becomes "to all appearances, the role of the bureaucracy." They depict the bureaucracy as having economic and political interests in maintaining its position and in consequence as being "involved as a special social entity in constant battles over the distribution of state income."[22] In a situation of high relative state autonomy, then, the bureaucracy figures as an important component in its own right in the determination of policy. And an analysis of the origins, interests and ideological orientation of bureaucrats permits some degree of understanding of the manner in which they make use of the freedom of action they enjoy within the relatively autonomous post-colonial state. However Ziemann and Lanzendorfer have aptly cautioned against attributing too great an importance to the bureaucracy or overrating their ability to choose state policy. At its base, they contend, the actions of the bureaucracy is determined by the reproductive demands of the society.

While Ziemann and Lanzendorfer posit status interests for the bureaucracy, other accounts suggest that the bureaucracy should best be regarded as a class. This is particularly so when the state has entered extensively into the economy as a direct participant so that the bureaucracy appears as agent of control of state enterprises. To quote Samoff, for instance, "where the state is dominant in the internal political economy and where the aspiring indigenous bourgeoisie is in most places weak, the bureaucracy becomes a class. Exercising the powers of ownership and responsible for maintaining the political conditions necessary for the reproduction of capitalist relations, the corporate group becomes a class-wielding power."[23]

The bureaucracy is all the more likely to govern as a class when formal political institutions are suppressed.[24] This holds similarity to what John Saul depicts as petty bourgeois politics. Samoff characterizes the bureaucracy on a class in an intermediary position between transnational capital and internal groups. Caught under conflicting pressures, its response reflects the variant possibilities which Saul suggested, moving "spasmotically in both directions, now allying with transnational capital to further its interests within the state, now forging a populist alliance with a mass base in order to wrest control from transnational capital."[25]

With reference to above Perez Sainz regards the formation of a state bourgeoisie as a necessary consequence of state capitalism. In his formulation the state bourgeoisie emerges as a distinct fraction of capital precisely because the reorientation entailed by state capitalism displaces the focus of accumulation from the private sphere to the state apparatus itself. The promotion of state capitalism is generally intended to sustain the inherited system where local capital is inadequate to the task. It is the characteristic result of adopting a nationalist strategy wherein the state directly assumes a critical role in accumulation, exercising a controlling intervention over the process.[26] This ascendency of state capitalism leads the transformation of the administrative bureaucracy into a state bourgeoisie. Amin[27] as well as Poulantzas[28] treat the state bourgeosie as a class establishing a specific place for itself through the state in existing relations of production. Peter Evans[29], however, accepts the existence of the state bourgeoisie in the peripheral states not as a replacement for the national industrial bourgeoisie but a sort of class fraction which participates in a common project with both the metropolitan bourgeoisie and the local bourgeoisie.

It is clear that the very extent of state intervention in a peripheral economy thrusts state personnel into centre stage. In controlling state enterprise they appear to determine directly the general orientation of the economy; moreover, being linked to the distributive mechanisms of state surplus, they appear to have particular facility for ensuring their own relative advantage. But whether their position allows their reproduction is not clear. Szentes declines to accept that it does. Arguing that the group he labels 'the elite', composed of civil servants, managers, administrators, bureaucrats, certain intellectuals and military officers, is not the owner of the means of production and thus lacks the capacity to ensure its privileged material position except by regulating distribution relations through political means, he suggests that in the long run it will be unable to maintain its own position in relative isolation from the productive process and thus is bound ultimately to lose the political powers which allow it to perpetuate its privileged position. For this reason, he contends that the state bourgeoisie cannot become a new and independent social class. It will ultimately merge either with the local industrial bourgeoisie as capitalist relations become generalized or alternatively will lose its elite character in a process of socialist development.

The Dominant Local Class as Transcending the boundary between state and civil society

A variation of the notion that the bureaucracy constitutes a distinct class is produced by Shivji[30] who puts forward the term bureaucratic bourgeoisie. This category denotes the ruling section of a larger class labeled, somewhat confusingly the petty bourgeoisie, the latter including prosperous farmers and businessmen, professionals and civil servants as well as shopkeepers and self-employed craftsmen. The petty bourgeoisie is identified as such for Shivji partly by the criterion of 'control or proximity to the state apparatus'. And it is apparently for this reason that bureaucracy is accorded by him a place as component of a larger class.

Similar reasoning seems to underlie other formulations which point to a new dominant class comprising an amalgam of individuals occupying very distinct positions within the production process and transcending both state and civil society. Sklar[31], for example, contends that new dominant class in 'non-industrial' societies comprises of businessmen, bureaucrats, politicians and members of the learned professionals. They become 'Managerial Bourgeoisie'. It is due to their very distinct positions within the production process and transcending both state and civil society. By using the concept of managerial bourgeoisie, Sklar refers to "the co-existence of a newly developing and dependent private enterprise sector with a preponderant yet projective public sector".

In such formulations, regarding state personnel as constituting a dominant class, as discussed above, the theorists have invariably used the same criteria. The criteria is based fundamentally on political rather than economic factors and specifically the accessor proximity to the state. Proponents of this position has thus postulated the existence of a new and distinct class which, even if still in some measure, subordinates to foreign capital moves into a dominant position in the peripheral societies. They have attributed its increasing dominance to its political prominence and also in its self promotion[32] through both state and private accumulation.

Nature of the Stae in the Post-Colonial Social Formations

The debate about the relationship of class to state in post-colonial social formations has clearly resulted in an array of interpretations and formulations. And while as has been indicated, the diversity is partly a function of the variability among the cases themselves, it also turns on the understanding of the very nature of class and of the state. It devolves on such issues as the following: the mechanism by which class interests are imposed on the state; the criteria for the specification of class dominance; whether metropolitan and indigenous bourgeoisie represent separate classes, fractions of a single class, or simply distinct interest groups, and the extent to which the post-colonial state can be conceptualized as merely a reflection of class forces and the class structure in which it is situated or as having an independent impact on society. Let us take up the issues in a more comprehensive manner.

The conception of the state that grew out of the predominance of dependency theory in the late 1960's was epitomised in Hamza Alavi's work on the overdeveloped post-colonial state. Alavi provided an important starting point for the analysis of the state in post-colonial societies – premising his arguments on the historical specificity of post-colonial societies, a specificity which arises from structural changes brought about by the colonial experience and alignment of classes and by the superstructures of political and administrative institutions which were established in that context and secondly from radical re-alignments of class forces which have been brought about in the post-colonial situation.

There are three points which define the crucial significance of the state in post-colonial societies that can be drawn from the analysis of Alavi and Saul. Two relate to the concepts advanced by Alavi, *viz.,* the notion of the 'overdeveloped' state and that of a new and relatively autonomous economic role of the state apparatus. To these John Saul adds a third feature, *viz.*, the special ideological function of the post-colonial state.

As for the first, Alavi holds that the post-colonial state dispenses with the mediation of politics because the state is overdeveloped, a superstructure capable of dominating all indigenous social forces. This allows aspects of the state itself (the military and/ or the bureaucracy) to play the dominant part in the state and above social classes.[33]

Alavi ascribed the genesis of this overdeveloped superstructure to the colonial past, where the task of carrying out the bourgeois revolution was undertaken by the metropolitan centre in the process of imposition of colonial rule. In that process it was necessary for the colonial power to create a state aparatus which was sufficiently powerful to subordinate the native social classes. Thus at the time of independence post-colonial state inherits the overdeveloped state apparatus and its institutionalized practices through which the operations of the indigenous social classes are regulated and controlled. In one of the later works, Alavi points out that he referred to this syndrome in the sense that "the excessive enlargement of powers of control and regulation that the state acquires extends far beyond the logic of what is necessary in the interests of the orderly functioning of the peripheral capitalist economies over which the state presides and specific needs of each of the dominant classes."[34]

With reference to above, a question has been raised about the attempt of relating the weak indigenous social classes with the overdeveloped colonial state in an unclear fashion. Why the colonial state was to be overdeveloped to dominate the indigenous social classes those who were basically weak? Colin Leys, in an auto critique, acknowledged the influence of Alavi on his earlier work, considers the concept of the overdeveloped state to be an empty category and argues against it from a theoretical as well as an empirical ground.

Colin Ley's theoretical argument against the concept of the overdeveloped state is directed towards this 'superficial' and misleading approach where the descriptive dimensions and activity of the state are the point of departure for the construction of any theory. Leys questions the whole way of approaching the question of the significance of the state, *i.e.* of starting out from its structure and scope. Leys contends that in order to understand the significance for any state of the class struggle, one must start from the class struggle, not the state.

At this place a word of caution may be raised. Even if we accept the validity of point, it offers no ready means of analyses as long as the classes are not easily identifiable, and as long as their struggles take place within the broadened context of a dependent economy and state.

As for the Leys' objections on the empirical ground about the notion of the overdeveloped state, he questions the argument that the inherited military and administrative machinery was excessive for the task of domination in the situation which existed by the time formal independence was achieved. In fact, Leys argues, it seems more plausible that the colonial state after the initial resistance to conquest has been overcome disposed of less military force than it would have required, if it had not been able to rely on reinforcement from the metropole or other parts of the colonial empire. Leys goes on to observe that the civil services and the armed forces have expanded more rapidly than earlier in the post-colonial phase. With regard to Tanzania, Leys finds the nation of the overdeveloped state even less plausible than on the Indian sub-continent for here – as Saul himself has pointed out – there were no strong classes to defend their interests in the colonial social formations.

A second complementary point also can be drawn from Alavi which explains the state's prominent place in post-colonial society. It is rooted not only in the colonial legacy but also in the contemporary production process. Post-colonial state assumes a new and relatively autonomous economic role, which is not paralleled in the classical bourgeoisie state, because the state in the post-colonial society directly approaches a very large part of the economic surplus and deploys it in bureaucratically directed economic activity in the name of promoting economic development. Thus in the name of 'development' the states under peripheral capitalism deploy "vast economic resources, often considerably exceeding the amount of private investment. Such resources are drawn in part from a proportion of the surplus value currently generated within the economy, but this is multiplied by resources drawn by borrowing from abroad."[35] Thus this scale of public expenditure state establishes an independent economic base and enables it to enjoy 'autonomous economic role'.

It remains to be said that despite enjoying a new and relatively autonomous economic role, the state's economic policies must remain within the framework and logic of peripheral capitalism otherwise state would invariably find itself in the grip of crisis. In this context Lanzendorfer and Ziemann have dubbed Alavi and Saul's analysis as predominantly politicised analysis, with a scanty recognition of international as well as national economic process. In fact, any material explanation total in real sense of the word, will necessarily have to include a description of the importance of world market integration for the peripheral nations (*i.e.* aspects of the internationalization of the capital) as well as the delimitation of the peripheral state as an actively economic intervening factor, relatively autonomous, but in the last instance hemmed in by international capital.

Lanzendorfer and Ziemann attributes the following economic functions to the peripheral states. First, the peripheral state does the function of linking the world market with the national economy by breaking down – as far as it is possible while maintaining the internal reproduction of the society – the political frontiers between the world market and the national economy, import of technology, foreign investment, etc. Secondly, the peripheral state does the function of securing the existence and expansion of the world market in the national economic area directed to the reproduction of both internationally operating capital and national capital oriented to the world market. Thirdly, the peripheral state secures the internal economic reproduction which is not automatically generated through the economic process. This is directed for instance to the extended reproduction of national capital based on the home market (promotion of industry, infrastructure, etc.). the reproduction of the moral and industrial labour force, as well as the independent and non-independent middle strata (wage policy, policy on food prices, etc.). Fourthly, the peripheral state maintains the structural heterogeneity, as a specific condition both for world market and national reproduction, against the process of disintegration in the non-capitalist area (through agrarian reforms etc.) and in the backward capitalist areas of the national economy (subsidies, price and wage policy).[36]

Coming back to the third feature which, according to Alavi and John Saul along with the above two, define the crucial significance of the state in the post-colonial social formations. This is the special ideological function of the state. Here Saul makes a pertinent distinction between the advanced capitalist societies and the post-colonial societies. According to him, "State's function of providing an ideological cement for the capitalist system is one which has gradually evolved in the core countries in step with their economic transformation. However, in post-colonial societies, this hegemonic position has to be created; and created within territorial boundaries which often apears quite artificial entities once the powerful force of direct colonial fiat has been removed."[37] Thus like Advanced Capitalism the peripheral capitalism too requires territorial unity and legitimacy which has to be created by the post-colonial state.

These three points, taken together, illuminate the omnipotent role of the post-colonial state. This centrality of the state, gets more pronounced as one takes Alavi's analysis of the class basis of the post-colonial formations. To quote Alavi, "The central position I wish to emphasize is that the state in the post-colonial society is not the instrument of a single class. It is relatively autonomous and it mediates the competing interests of the three propertied classes – the metropolitan bourgeoisie, the indigenous bourgeisie, and the landed class while at the same time acting on behalf of all of them in order to preserve tne social order in which their interests are embedded, namely, the institution of private property and the capitalist mode as the dominant mode of production."[38]

Pertinently, Alavi does not abandon the conception of a class basis of the political power and the state, in favour of a "free floating autonomous state with its own independent logic and will."[39] Moreover, according to him, state does not act only in response to the expressed demands of the economically dominant classes and only at their behest, rather it presides over the working of the peripheral capitalist economy in accordance with its internal logic. State while recognising the 'structural imperative' of peripheral capitalism, also has to secure the necessary conditions for the reproduction of the social order in which economically dominant classes are situated.

State Policy as Limited and Influenced by Class Forces

Clearly a state or a regime would not suffer immediate demise should it bypass the limits imposed by its structural context; nor should inability to ensure reproduction at a sustained level lead immediately to social dissolution. However, the limits are real enough and the exceeding of them must soon show up in negative growth, increasing balance of payment problems, and the like. Economic structure, to reiterate, implies a ceratin class structure, so that structural limits on policy have as their counterpart a pattern of indirect pressure of class forces, or, as Hamilton states, structural constrains are based on direct or indirect power relations.[40] If the post-colonial state continues to rely on metropolitan capital (to a greater or lesser degree), it frequently does so because in the short run reproduction is impossible without such reliance. In this manner metropolitan bourgeoisie exerts a clear class pressure – often definitive – on the state, even if in an indirect or passive sense.

Nor is the impact of foreign capital merely indirect or passive. When the state exceeds the limits describing metropolitan bourgeoisie's control, a very active class response is invariably forthcoming. The impact of this class is often highly political and often extremely direct, irrespective of its position with respect to local democratic institutions.

Exceeding of limits established by an existing class structure does not elicit a response only from metropolitan bourgeoisie. For policy which threatens the reproduction of urban workers, the unemployed, or the peasantry is also likely to bring forth very dramatic expression of interests. However it depends on the level of consciousness and organization of these subordinate classes as well as the nature of political conjuncture.[41]

While structure sets limits, there is generally a wide range of policy options existing within these limits, not all of which are necessarily optimal for bourgeoisie in general nor metropolitan bourgeoisie in particular. To some extent the choice among options as Ziemann and Lanzendorfer have noted, is influenced by the status interests of the bureaucracy. It is also influenced by the nature of prevailing institutional structures (*i.e.* the limitations imposed by constitutional procedures and provisions). Then the policy is also influenced by actively exerted class pressures. Politics indeed may be regarded as the active expression of class interests; bourgeois democracy provides an institutional framework for facilitating such expression.

It is the indigenous classes, through the mechanism of the franchise, which have access to the state through the legitimized representative institutions. And it is with regard to this mechanism, that independence has had a profound effect. The system provides a means of determining which class actors are eligible to occupy representative bodies and, moreover, who is able to gain governmental position. Independence has thus changed the state of candidates capables of taking charge of the state.

If instituional change with independence altered some mechanisms through which class pressure is expressed or articulated, it left others intact. For active class pressure is of course not limited to that following legislative channels. It occurs as well in the form of pressure group activity – whether lobbying or bribing or whatever. In this regard in particular, if metropolitan bourgeoisie is excluded from access to the state through franchise it is hardly excluded from exerting other forms of direct influence. Thus it can be presumed that independence as such did not bring much change in the identity of the economically dominant classes. Moreover, structural continuity ensured that the post-colonial state remained embedded in a society in which the capitalist mode was ascendant. However if the end of colonialism effected a change in political relations, did it thereby imply a change in the identity of the politically dominant class? An answer requires some exploration of the relationship between economic and political dominance.

Class Dominance – Economic and Political

It has already been noted that reproduction of capitalist societies necessarily involves reproduction of bourgeoisie's dominant position *vis-a-vis* other classes. The policy of the state as an institution whose fundamental object is societal reproduction necessarily reflects this dominance. This is not to imply that the state serves as direct 'instrument' of bourgeoisies, such that each component of policy is discernible as directly in accordance with the interests of capital. It merely suggests that on balance, if the social formation is to be reproduced as capitalist, that is, incorporating existing class antagonisms – it must maintain the dominance of the capitalist class and thus on balance reflect the essential interests of that class. To this degree there is an evident and strong relationship between economic position and political effects. Yet at the same time there is no necessary identity between the class which holds political power and directly rules and that which is economically dominant.[42]

It is evident that while one class, *e.g.*, the bourgeoisie as a whole, may be regarded as economically dominant and therefore exercising indirectly or directly political dominance or control, a single section or fraction of it may be judged to the ruling or governing element, being most active in the political process and indeed holding the reins of government. At the same time it would seem possible that a single section or fraction of the politically dominant class because of its structural location or because of its more active role in the political process – may exercise some measure of dominance over other sections of the class.

The economically dominant class is generally perceived as a class whose reproductive needs ultimately determine the overall economic structure of social formation, the essential course of development, and the ascendency or undermining of other classes or class fractions. Political dominance, however, is to be judged in terms of the output of the State and therein the determination of specific policy within limits set by the general reproductive needs of the economically dominant class. At one level as indicated above, there is a necessary correspondence between the economically and politically dominant class. But the possibility exists for a section of the economically dominant class, through its involvement in the political process and its direct control of government, to be on balance a relatively greater beneficiary of policy.

Thus control of the state through control of Government provides a tool by which a class or section of a class can strengthen its position, *vis-a-vis* other sections of the same class and of other classes. To this degree the state may be regarded as having an effect on the class struggle within the peripheral structure. Yet whether such an effect is independent of class forces is another matter. Patankar and Omvedt reject the notion that the state is a determinant as well as a product of the class struggle, arguing that the state does not exist separately to be a determinant as well as a product of the class struggle, arguing that the state does not exist separately to be a determinant and that the state structure as such does not act.[43] However if the state is not independent of the class situation in which it is embedded, this is not to say that its policies do not have an objective and often critical effect on class struggle, including the rate of ascendency of certain classes or class fractions. The notion of relative state autonomy, moreover implies that, while hardly acting in a class vacuum, state personnel experience relative degrees of direction from class forces; the sphere of freedom of choice of state personnel is thus a variable and involves differing potential for effects neither directly dictated by class forces nor attributable to specific and immediate class pressure.

Concluding Observation

Having established some general theoretical premises, it would be pertinent to move to the more concrete situation of post-colonial states. What, for instance, in the post-colonial period has been the concrete identity of what can be abstractly labeled the economically dominant class, the politically dominant class, the governing or ruling class, the class in change of the state, etc.? In the course of the paper, bourgeoisie has been alluded with the identity of being the economically dominant class. It has been suggested that it is the interests of this class which have been given preponderance by the post-colonial state as indicated by the nature of state policy. Moreover, in most of the circumstances, it is a section of the bourgeoisie, namely metropolitan bourgeoisie, whose interests appear to be pre-eminently safeguarded.

However the pertinent question confronts the theorists with regard to the position of metropolitan bourgeoisie *vis-a-vis* indigenous bourgeoisie. Is metropolitan bourgeoisie a separate class or is a fraction of the 'whole' bourgeoisie within post-colonial formations, or what?

To reiterate, in any capitalist economy, bourgeoisie shares a certain commonality of interests whether metropolitan or indigenous. Yet, the fact of nationality or national identity, so closely intertwined with the historical emergence of capital, does bear on the specific interests of indigenous bourgeoisie and metropolitan bourgeoisie and does entail a conflict of interests between them. The issue in question involves the disposal of indigenously produced surplus. In general terms, it is in the interest of indigenous capitalists to retain surplus for local use and reinvestment, whereas metropolitan capitalists may well wish to export profits produced in their local enterprises. In line with the more global strategy of the multinational companies, it is the post-colonial state which serves to set the terms of surplus disposal, and these terms in turn reflect the relative political as well as economic power of indigenous as opposed to metropolitan bourgeoisie.

In a general and perhaps in a over-simplified sense metropolitan bourgeoisie can be perceived as occupying a position of relative economic dominance within the capitalist class of a peripheral economy. Nonetheless the question mark remains over its political role. It may be relatively politically dominant in most of the cases, in the sense of its interests enjoying pre-eminence in state policy but this cannot be generalized. It is conceivable that metropolitan bourgeoisie can enjoy a predominance in the political process, but this is highly unlikely, particularly as it is formally excluded from party politics (and thus its predominance would have to follow exclusively from such activities as control through international institutions).

It is evident that at a minimum, independence entailed disruption to the metropolitan bourgeoisie not least through altering the mechanisms by which its political role could be exercised. This, in combination with the increased pressure from the subordinate indigenous bourgeoisie, leads to the post-colonial state enjoying a considerable degree of autonomy.

References

1. Ralph Miliband, 'Marxism and Politics', London, Oxford University Press, 1977, p. 29.
2. *Ibid.*, p. 106.
3. Hamza Alavi, 'Class and State' in H. Gardezi and J. Rashid (eds.) 'Pakistan: The Roots of Dictatorship', London, Zed Press, 1983, p. 43-4.
4. A.G. Frank, 'Crisis in the Third World', London, Heinemann Educational Books Ltd., 1981, p. 233.
5. Nelson Kasfir (ed.) 'State and Class in Africa', Introduction, London, Frankcass, 1984, p. 1.

6. Richard Higgot, 'Political Development Theory', New York, Croom Helms, 1983, p. 65.

7. Michelae Von Freyhold, 'The Post-colonial State and its Tanzanian Version', Review of African Political Economy, 8 (Jan-April), 1977, pp. 81-88.

8. Bharat Patankar and Gail Omvedt, 'Bourgeois State in Post-colonial Social Formations', Economic and Political Weekly, Dec. 1977, p. 2165.

9. N. Swainson, 'The Rise of a National Bourgeoisie in Kenya', Review of African Political Economy', 8 (Jan-April), 1977, pp. 39-40.

10. Colin Leys, "Capital Accumulation, Class Formation and Dependence: The significance of the Kenyan Case", the Socialist Register, 1978, p. 253.

11. Bjorn Beckman, 'Imperialism and Capitalist Transformation: A Critique of a Kenyan Debate', Review of African Political Economy, 19 (Sep-Dec), 1980, p. 59.

12. Hamza Alavi, 'Character of State in Pakistan' in V.D. Chopra (ed.)., 'Studies in Indo-Pak Relations', New Delhi, Patriot Publishers, 1984, p. 69.

13. *Ibid.*, p. 45.

14. Mahmood Mamdani, 'Class Struggles in Uganda', Review of African Political Economy, 4 (Sept-Dec.), 1977.

15. Claude Ake, 'Revolutionary Pressures in Africa', London, 1978, p. 61.

16. V.I. Stains et. al. 'The Role of the State in Socio-Economic Reforms in Developing Countries', Moscow Progress, 1976, p. 34.

17. T. Szentes, 'The Political Economy of Underdevelopment', Budapest, Akadamiai Kiada, 1971, p. 318.

18. Ian Roxborough, 'Theories of Underdevelopment', London, Macmillan, 1979, pp. 72-73.

19. John Saul, 'The State in Post-colonial Societies', Tanzania's in his book, 'The State and Revolution in Eastern Africa', London, Heinemann Educational Book Ltd., 1979, p. 11.

20. Hamza Alavi, 'The State in Post-colonial Societies' in Kathleen Gough and Hari Sharma (eds.) 'Imperialism and Revolution in South Asia', New York, Monthly Review Press, 1973, p. 148.

21. Ralph Miliband, N.1, p. 108.

22. Ziemann and Lanzendorfer, 'The State in Peripheral Societies'; Ralph Miliband & J. Saville (eds.), The Socialist Register, 1977, p. 165.

23. Joel Samoff, 'Class, Class Conflict and the State in Africa', Political Science Quarterly, 27 (Spring), 1982, p. 125.

24. *Ibid.*, p. 126.

25. *Ibid.*, p. 127.

26. Perez Sainz, 'Towards A Conceptualization of State Capitalism in the Periphery', The Insurgent Sociologist, 9 (Spring), 1980, p. 59-67.

27. Samir Amin, 'Unequal Development: An Essay on the Social Formations of Peripheral Capitalism', New York, Monthly Review Press, 1976, p. 346.

28. Nicos Poulantzas, 'Political Power and Social Classes', London, New Left Books, 1975, p. 334.

29. Peter Evans, 'Dependent Development: The Alliance of Multinational State and Local Capital in Brazil', Princeton, Princeton Univ. Press, 1979, pp. 46-47.

30. ISSA Shivji, 'Class Struggles in Tanzania', London, Heinemann, 1976, p. 88.
31. Richard Sklar, 'The Nature of Class Domination in Africa', The Journal of Modern African Studies, 17 (4), 1979, p. 537.
32. Ralph Miliband, N. 1, p. 108-9.
33. Hamza Alavi, No. 20, p. 147.
34. Hamza Alavi, 'Character of State in Pakistan', in VD Chopra (ed.), 'Studies in Indo-Pak Relations', New Delhi, Patriot Publishers, 1984, p. 43.
35. Hamza Alavi, 'State and Class' in Shanin and Alavi (eds.) 'Sociology of Developing Societies', London, Macmillan, 1982, p. 303.
36. Adapted from Lanzendorfer and Ziemann, No. 22, pp. 160-162.
37. John Saul, N. 15, p. 170.
38. Hamza Alavi, 'The State in Post-colonial Societies', No. 20, p. 148.
39. Alavi, 'Character of State in Pakistan', N. 12, p. 69.
40. Nora Hamilton, 'The Limits of State Autonomy : Post-revolutionary Mexico', Princeton, Princeton University Press, 1982, p. 283.
41. Hamza Alavi, N. 35, p. 306.
42. Nicos Poulantzas, N. 28, pp. 249-50.
43. Bharat Patankar and Gail Omvedt, 'The Bourgeois State in Post-Colonial Formations', The Insurgent Sociologist, 9 (Spring), 1980, pp. 23-38.

CHAPTER III

MARXIAN ANALYSIS OF PRE-COLONIAL AND COLONIAL INDIAN SOCIETY

Karl Marx's concept of Asiatic society and the Asiatic mode of production has been at the core of Marxist debates concerning Asia – and much of the rest of the non-European world – for more than a hundred years.[1] India, in fact, bulked large in Marx's thought in the most creative period of his activity, from 1853 to 1867[2]. Karl Marx and Friedrich Engels, for the first time, became interested in the analysis of Indian society[3] in 1853 as a consequence of their journalistic criticisms of British Foreign Policy. Marx in collaboration with Engels wrote his pieces on historical sociology of India which were published in 'New York Daily Tribune'. The significant ones among them have been, 'The British rule in India', and 'The Future Results of the British Rule in India.'[4] Marx was intensely interested in the uprising of 1857 and contributed regularly to various journals on the Indian Question at that stage. Marxist concept of pre-colonial Indian society was influenced by James Mill (History of British India), by John Stuart Mill (Principles of Political Economy), by Tavernier (Travels in India, Volume 1), by Francois Bernier (Travels in the Mogul Empire), by Mark Wilks (Historical Sketches of the South of India), and by Richard Jones (An Essay on the Distribution of Wealth and the Sources of Taxation). Marx and Engels also undertook a careful reading of English Parliamentary Papers for writing their articles. Thus most of the elements that went into the making of Marx and Engels' understanding of Asia's history had been in circulation in Europe for varying lengths of time.[5] The theme taken up by Marx in his journalistic articles continued to recur in both Marx and Engels' mature writings – 'Grundrisse', Capital, Vol. I, 'Pre-capitalist Economic Formations' and 'Anti-Duhring'.

However, Marx and Engels failed to work out a coherent theory of Asiatic society.[6] Even a collection of all direct and indirect references in the Writings of Marx and Engels, to the Asiatic mode of Production, the Oriental form etc. fail to add up to a clear and consistent picture in this regard.[7] This may be partly attributed to the fact that both Marx and

Engels remained till the end of their life, in search of a comprehensive and systematic formulation which could have explained the complex pre-capitalist economic formations existing in the Asiatic society. As Irfan Habib argues, the failure of Marx to publish in his own life-time anything out of the manuscripts of the Pre-capitalist Economic Formations should 'reasonably be regarded as a token of his own unwillingness to present as his final opinion what were clearly tentative or speculative points.'[8] Moreover, Marx and Engels were primarily involved in the analysis and comprehension of the capitalist society of the nineteenth century. Asiatic Society was studied mainly in order to find out how the Capitalism of the 19th century of Europe had come into being. To quote Heinz Lubasz, "What the concept Asiatic mode of 'Production' conceptualizes is not Asian society, which Marx knew very little about and never attempted to theorise, but the hypothetical origins of modern bourgeois society, which Marx knew a lot about and spent a life-time theorising."[9] Thus the Marxian concept of Asiatic mode of Production had a negative importance in Marxism in that its main theoretical function was not to analyse Asiatic society but to explain the rise of capitalism in Europe within a comparative framework.[10]

In their earlier articles, Marx and Engels held the age-old village system as the most distinctive characteristic of India. Indeed, the village community seems to have provided Marx with an important clue to the hidden dynamic of India's long distance history. As Diptendra Banerjee puts it, "For those who do not see a famine of facts and logic in the Marxian notion of the Asiatic mode of Production as a distinctive pre-capitalist system of production, the Indian or Oriental Village Community seems to have been the life-blood, as it were, of the Asiatic mode of Production itself, the Central focus of its very life-style."[11] The Indian villages have been called 'stereotyped Primitive Forms as they preserved their ancient structure. As these villages were held together by ties of consangunities, so they were also labeled as 'Family Communities' by Engels. These village communities had 'stagnatory' and 'passive sort of existence'. This stagnancy was primarily due to the absence of private property, particular private ownership of land. Periodic changes in the political organisation of Indian society from dynastic struggles and military conquest could not bring about radical changes in economic organisation. This was due to the fact that the ownership of land and organisation of agricultural activities remained with the oriental state as the real landlord. The static nature of Indian Village Communities was dependent on the coherence of the village system which, combining agriculture and handicrafts, was economically self-sufficient. This 'domestic union of agricultural and manufacturing pursuits' and 'an unalterable division of labour' (besides 'possession in common of the land') became the basis of these self-sufficient village communities which "existed with a given scale of low conveniences, almost without intercourse with other villages, without the desires and efforts indispensable to social advance." These communities were, for geographical and climatic reasons,[12] dependent on irrigation which required a centralized administrative apparatus to coordinate and develop large scale hydraulic works.[13] Despotism as well as socio-economic stagnation were thus explained by the dominant role of the oriental state in public works and the self-sufficienty and isolated nature of the Indian Village system. All these elements together eliminated the possibility of any basic changes in the socio-economic structure for centuries until India's colonisation by Britain.

Marx and 'Engels conceded that at first glance there might seem something attractive about India's simple and economically self-sufficing village communities. However, Marx condemned the closed nature of these communities. He criticised these societies also because they made man subject to nature rather than master of his own destiny. To quote Marx: "... these idyllic village communities ... had always been the solid foundation of oriental despotism ... they restrained the human mind within the smallest possible compass, making it the unresisting tool of superstition, enslaving it beneath traditional rules, depriving it of all grandeur and historical energies. We must not forget the barbarian egotism which, concentrating on some miserable patch of land, had quietly witnessed the ruin of empires, the perpetration of unspeakable cruelties, the massacre of the population of large towns, with no other consideration bestowed upon them than of natural events, itself the helpless prey of any aggressor who deigned to notice it at all. We must not forget that this undignified, stagnatory and vegetative life, that the passive sort of existence, evoked on the other part, in contradistinction, wild, aimless, unbounded forces of destruction, and rendered murder itself as religious rite in Hindustan. We must not forget that these little communities were contaminated by distinctions of caste and by slavery, that they subjected man to external circumstances. Instead of elevating man the sovereign of circumstances, that they transformed a self-developing social state into never changing natural destiny..."[14]

This preliminary sketch of Pre-colonial Indian society was modified and extended by Marx and Engels to come out with a far more complex view of the Asiatic Mode of Production in their mature works. In the Grundrisse, Marx for the first time distinguished urban history of the oriental society from the European society. In feudal European society, the politically independent cities became the locations for the growth of the production of exchange values, which in turn heralded the growth of a bourgeoisie as well as industrial capitalism. On the other hand in the Asiatic cities were the artificial creation of the despotic state. For Marx, the existence of towns and cities that were no more than military camps 'superimposed on the real economic structure'. Cities have been termed 'Princely Camps'. Marx in his mature works 'Grundrisse' and 'Capital', Volume I, attributed special emphasis on the communal ownership of land by self-sufficient village communities which were the real basis of the social unity represented by the state.

In Grundrisse, the notion of Asiatic mode of production thus emerged as one form of communal appropriation which could, in principle, occur even outside the Asiatic society. The characteristics of the Asiatic mode of production, among others, were its resistance to change of any kind and the absence of internal contradictions to undermine it. The similar theme appeared in capital, volume one, where Marx returned to theorize about the existence of the village commune, absence of private property and communal ownership, and 'a self-sustaining cycle of production, unity of agriculture and the handicrafts'. These factors provided the foundation for the oriental despotism and social immutability. In capital, it is the simplicity of the 'natural economy' of the Asiatic village communities which defines the essential feature of Asiatic stability, as Marx puts it, 'the secret of the unchangingness of Asiatic societies'. The surplus product of Asiatic economy was collected by the despotic state in the form of tribute or tax that, at one stage in Marx's thinking, had assumed the characteristics of rent.[15]

The diverse features of Asiatic society, mentioned above, enabled Marx and Engels to place the station annexs of Asiatic society in relation to the European development. To reiterate, Marx was primarily interested in the study of the development of capitalism and so his study of the Asiatic society enabled him to identify those factors in European feudalism which were conducive to capitalist development. Asiatic soicety was attributed with an overdeveloped state apparatus and an underdeveloped civil society.[16] In European Feudal society, civil society held primacy over the state. Moreover the essential social ingredients essential for the rise of bourgeoisie, *i.e.* free market, private property, guild structure and bourgeois law system were absent due to the dominance of despotic state over civil society. Significantly, the absence of the institution of private property ruled out the development of social classes as agents of social change. Thus Asiatic society was a society where "the great split into an exploiting and an exploited class had not yet occurred" and as such Engels[17] did not include its history among the epochs of civilization.[18] Thus the characteristic of change lessness in India's Pre-colonial history was put in contrast by Marx and Engels to the rapidly changing states of historical development in Europe – slavery, feudalism and modern capitalism.[19] The caste system which Marx and Engels regarded as a primitive form of class relationship was mentioned only in a passing manner and in any case it was relevant only in case of India.

In the absence of internal mechanism of social change, one implication of Marx and Engels' analysis of Asiatic Society was that British Colonialism had become an 'unconscious tool of history' in bringing about "a fundamental revolution in the social state of Asia" which would rid the Asiatic society of the muck of all ages, however, painful to its people the process might be. In their 'New York Daily Tribune' articles, Marx and Engels argued that the British had torn apart the village communities with their 'stagnatory' and 'passive sort of existence'. The self-sufficiency as well as the isolation of the oriental economy became extinct. Marx formulated British Capital's 'double mission' theory – a mission destructive as well as regenerating. As Marx said, "England has to fulfil a double mission in India: one destructive, the other regenerating – the annihilation of the old Asiatic society and the laying of the material foundations of western society in Asia."[20]

With reference to above Avineri has attributed to Marx the following thesis: "Just as the horrors of industrialisation are dialectically necessary for the world revolution of the proletariat since without them the countries of Asia will not be able to emancipate themselves from their stagnant backwardness."[21] Avineri goes on to argue, 'the direct corollary of this (the conflict between Marx's "European-oriented philosophy of history' and 'the non-dialectical stagnant nature of the Asiatic mode of Production') would be that Marx would have to welcome European penetration in direct proportion to its intensity : the more direct the European control of any society in Asia, the greater the chances for the overhauling of its structure and its ultimate incorporations into bourgeois, and hence later into socialist society.'[22]

Marx and Engels, however, shifted rapidly from the regenerative aspects of British colonialism to its destructive aspects. "As the facts concerning colonialism accumulated", H.B. Davis points out "Marx's enthusiasm for capitalism as a transforming instrument cooled."[23] To their later writings, Marx and Engels noted several structural features of British colonialism that negated economic development in the sense that it started a process of de-industrialisation and transformed Asiatic economy into an appendage of the economy of the metropolitan societies.[24] Marx noted, "By ruining handicraft production in other countries, machinery forcibly converts them into fields for the supply of its raw material. In this way East India was compelled to produce cotton, wool, hemp, jute and Indigo for Great Britain ... A New and International division of labour, a division suited to the requirements of the chief centres of modern industry springs up, and converts one part of the globe into a chiefly agricultural field of production, for supplying the other part which remains a chiefly industrial field."[25] Marx also observed that "the production itself ... was changed according to its greater or minor suitableness for exportation."[26] That is, dragged into the orbit of capitalist world trade, with a major portion of its productive forces either destroyed or refashioned to suit the demands of colonial capital, the Asiatic economy was forced to acquire a satellite character.

Marx strongly condemned the plundering of wealth to Britain, one of the formidable obstacles to the bourgeois development of India: Karl Marx in a letter to Danilso wrote: 'What the English take from them (the Indian) annually in the form of rent, dividends for railways useless to the Hindus, pensions for military and civil servicemen, for Afganistan and other wars, etc. etc. what they take from them without any equivalent and quite apart from what they appropriate to themselves annually within India – speaking only of the value of the commodities the Indians have gratuitously and annually to send over to England – it amounts to more than the total sum of income of the 60 millions of agricultural and industrial labourers of India ! This is a bleeding process with a vengeance!'[27] In the similar vein Marx revised his opinion about the nature of Zamindari and ryotwari systems. He had earlier welcomed that land settlement act for introducing private property in land but later described the 'exclusive proprietary rights claimed by the Talukdars and Zamindars' as "an incubus on the real cultivators of the soil and the general improvement of the country."[28] In 1881 Marx while criticising Sir Henry Maine,[29] observed that "the extinction of the communal ownership of land was only an act of English vandalism which pushed the indigenous people not forward but backward."[30] There is no doubt that Marx had outgrown his earlier optimism about the revolutionary role of British colonialism.[31]

Marx and Engels spoke of the colonial character of Irish Society and economy. The essence of colonialism in Ireland, they said, was the subordination of the Irish to the British economy and the transformation of Ireland into an agrarian appendage of Industrial Britain. Engels said about Irish situation, "Irish history shows what a misfortune it is for one nation to have subjugated another."[32] In early 1870, he observed, "The more I study the subject the clearer it is to me that Ireland has been stunted in its development by the English invasion and thrown centuries back."[33] This underdevelopment of the Irish economy took place as Ireland was used as a supplier of raw materials, a market for manufactured goods, and a place for the safe investment of capital in land. Besides these, Ireland also served as a supplier of cheap labour.

For a long time, Marx and Engels had thought that a colonial revolution could only be a sequel to the revolution in the metropolis. Thus Marx said, "It would be possible to overthrow the Irish regime by English working class ascendency." However, he later changed his mind, "Deeper study has now convinced me of the opposite", Marx went on to say that for the English Proletariat, "the national emancipation of Ireland is no question of abstract justice or humanitarian sentiment but the first condition of their own social emancipation."[34] Similarly in the context of India, Engels wrote in a letter to Kautsky about the countries which are "merely subjugated ... must be taken over for the time-being by the Proletariat and led as rapidly as possible towards independence. How this process will develop, it is difficult to say. India will perhaps, indeed very probably make a revolution, and as a proletariat in process of self-emancipation cannot make only colonial wars, it would have to be allowed to run its course, it would not pass without all sorts of destruction, of course, but that sort of thing's inseparable from any revolution ... But as to what social and political phases these countries will then have to pass through before they likewise arrive at a socialistic organization. I think we today can advance only rather idle hypotheses. One thing alone is certain : the victorious proletariat can force no blessings of any kind on any foreign nation without undermining its own victory by so doing."[35] Engels thus clearly saw the historical nexus between the two revolutions on two different levels, that is, the anti-capitalist revolution in the European metropolis and the anti-imperialist anti-feudal revolution in the colonies.

However, Marx and Engels did not leave behind any 'theory' of a colonial revolution. To reiterate, what Marx and Engels wrote about Indian society and other colonial societies was concerned primarily with the cognitive problem of analysing a society and economy so differently structured from the European. Moreover Marx along with Engels had indeed foreseen the possibility of a capitalist transformation of India under the British imperialism, but only as an abstract possibility. Later, as has been discussed above, there was a distinct shift in their understanding on the Colonial problem. Thus Marx and Engels never made any predictions about the future of the Asiatic society, contrary to the common academic prejudice.[36]

References

1. These debates have ranged from issues of immediate and vital political significance — Strategies of revolution, directions of social and economic development — to broad questions concerning the interpretation of world history and the study of economic anthropology. For a brief Introduction to these debates, refer Helene Carrere d'Encausse and Stuart R. Schram, 'Marxism and Asia' London, 1969.
2. Daniel Thorner, 'Marx on India and the Asiatic mode of Production', Contributions to Indian Sociology, Vol. 6 (1964), p. 33.
3. Marx designated Indian society as the 'Asiatic Society' or the 'Asiatic System' in articles written on India in 1853. Perhaps for the first time the expression, 'the Asiatic Mode of Production' was used by him in the Economic Manuscripts of 1857-1859, published afterwards under the title 'Grundrisse'. Suniti Kumar Ghosh, 'Marx on India', Monthly Review, January, 1984.
4. Karl Marx, 'Articles on India', Bombay, Progress, 1951, pp. 21-29, 66-73.
5. Harbans Mukhia, 'Marx on Pre-colonial India' in Diptendra Banerjee (ed.) 'Marxian Theory and the Third World', New Delhi, Sage Publications, 1985, p. 173.
6. For Critique of the Concept of Asiatic Mode of Production by Social Scientists sympathetic to Marxian Theory as a whole, one may mention the following — Daniel Thorner, 'Marx on India and the Asiatic Mode of Production', N.2; Bipan Chandra, 'Karl Marx, His Theories of Asian Societies, and Colonial Rule', Review 5 (1981), pp. 13-93; and Irfan Habib, 'The Agrarian System of Mughal India' (Bombay and London, (1963) — among those dealing with India in particular, on an empirical basis. On the theoretical side one may mention Perry Anderson, The Asiatic Mode of Production', in his 'Lineages of the Absolutist State' (London, 1974), pp. 462-549, and Barry Hindess and Paul Q. Hirst, 'Pre-capitalist Modes of Production' (London, 1975) and Lawrence Krader, 'The Asiatic Mode of Production' (Assez 1975), pp. 304-17.
7. Daniel Thorner, N. 1, p. 34.
8. Irfan Habib, 'Problems of Marxist Historical Analysis', in Dr. K. Mathew Kurient (ed.) 'India — State and Society', Bombay, Orient Longman, p. 21.
9. Heinz Lubasz, 'Marx's Concept of the Asiatic Mode of Production' in Diptendra Banerjee, 'Marxian Theory and the Third World', New Delhi, Sage, 1985, p. 108.

10. Bryan S. Turner, 'Asiatic Society', in Tom Bottomore (ed.) 'A Dictionary of Marxist Thought', Oxford Blackwell, 1983, p. 36.
11. Diptendra Banerjee, 'Marx and the 'Original, Form of India's Village Community' in Diptendra Banerjee, N. 5, p. 133.
12. Marx and Engels, 'Selected Correspondence' Quoted in Kandadi Seshadri, 'Marxism and Indian Polity', New Delhi, Peoples Publishing House, 1988, p. 86.
13. Wittfogel in his book, 'Oriental despotism' discussed the implications of centralised management of irrigation in the social structure of China in an empirical manner. The theoretical inspiration for Wittforgel's study of hydraulic economy in his Wirtschaft and Gesellschaft Chinas came from Weber's application of the notion of 'Patrimonial bureaucracy' to Chinese history. Karl A. Wittfogel, 'Oriental Despotism: A Comparative Study of Total Power', New Haven, Yale University Press, 1963.
14. K. Marx, 'The British Rule in India', New York Daily Tribune, June 25, 1853. Cited in Daniel Thorner, N. 2, p. 40.
15. Harbans Mukhia, 'Marx on Precolonial India', N. 5, p. 173.
16. Bryan S. Turner, 'Asiatic Society', N. 10, p. 33-34.
17. E. Engels, 'The Origin of the Family, Private Property and the State' quoted in Harbans Mukhia, N. 5, p. 180.
18. Eric Hobsbawm explains the reason behind Engel's silence over the Asiatic mode of production, while talking of 'the three epoches of civilisation' — namely slavery, feudalism and modern bourgeoisie — by saying that it was omitted by Engels 'as belonging to the Pre-history of civilization'. E.J. Hobsbawm (ed.), 'Introduction', in, 'Karl Marx: Pre-capitalist Economic Formations', New York, 1971, p. 51n.
19. "The history of hydraulic (*i.e.* oriental) society suggests that class struggle, far from being a chronic disease of all mankind, is the luxury of multi-centred and open (*i.e.* west European) societies'. Karl Wittfogel, 'Oriental Despotism: A Comparative Study of Total Power', Quoted by Irfan Habib, 'Problems of Marxist Historical Analysis', N. 8, p. 24.
20. Karl Marx, quoted in Martin Carnoy, 'The State and Political Theory', Princeton, Princeton University Press, 1983, p. 174.
21. Shlomo Avineri (ed), 'Karl Marx on Colonialism and Modernization', New York, Double day, 1968, p. 12.
22. *Ibid.*, p. 18.
23. Horace Davis, 'Capital and Imperialism: A Landmark in Marxist Theory', Monthly Review, September 1967, p. 18.
24. Interest in the Asiatic Mode of Production was one aspect of a more general trend in Marxism to produce concepts of Dependency, Uneven development and Underdevelopment in order to grasp the effects of capitalist expansion on Peripheral economics.
25. Karl Marx, 'Capital', Vol. I, Moscow, Progress, 1974, pp. 424-25.
26. Karl Marx to N.F. Danielson, Ap.10, 1879, in Marx and Engels, 'Selected Correspondence', Moscow, Progress, 1965, p. 318.
27. Marx to N.F. Danielson, Feb. 19, 1881, in *Ibid.*, p. 337.
28. Marx and Engels, 'The First Indian War of Independence, 1857-1859, Moscow, Progress Publishers, p. 103.

29. Lawrence Krader, 'The Asiatic Mode of Production' in Town Bottomore and Patrick Goode (ed.) 'Readings in Marxist Sociology', Oxford, Clarendon Press, 1983, p. 80.
30 K. Marx quoted in Morin Kenzo, 'Marx and Underdevelopment', Annals of the Institute of Social Science, No. 19, 1978, p. 50.
31. Earlier Marx had believed that the ruin and devastation caused by British Colonialism was a terrible but necessary price for 'the only social revolution ever heard in Asia.'
32. Cited in Lenin, 'The Right of Nations to Self-Determination', 'Collected Works', Vol. 20, Moscow, Progress, 1972, p. 438.
33. Engels to Marx, January 19, 1870, in Marx and Engels, 'On Colonialism', Moscow, Progress, 1965, p. 331.
34. Marx to S. Meyer and A. Vogt, April 9, 1870 in *Ibid.*, p. 335.
35. F. Engels to Kautsky in Marx and Engels, 'Selected Correspondence', Moscow, Progress, 1965, p. 351.
36. Marx said that he did not enjoy preparing like Comte, "recipes for the kitchen in which the future is cooked'. Sudipta Kaviraj, 'Marxian Theory and Analysis of Indian Politics', in 'A Survey of Research in Political Science', Volume 4, New Delhi, Allied Publishers Pvt. Ltd., 1984, p. 142.

CHAPTER IV

CLASS AND STATE IN POST-COLONIAL INDIAN SOCIETY

The State has grown increasingly important in every society, from advanced capitalist to the post-colonial societies. Its importance is manifested in every aspect of society – not just politics, but in economic and in ideology.[1] No wonder, the state is once again in focus. Once abandoned by the structural functional theorists in the post-Second World War years, the state has been brought back[2] in as a major subject of study, more so in the context of the post-colonial societies by the Marxist social scientists. Underlying this revival is a concern with the role of the post-colonial state in the accumulation process and in developing and expanding capitalist production relations, in consolidating capitalist ruling classes, which revolves around the axes of state autonomy and 'state capacity'.[3]

The issues which the Marxist theorists have posed in the renewal of state theory concern the nature of autonomy of the post-colonial state from the societal forces. Is the post-colonial state in autonomous actor or is it subordinated to the interest of the ruling class (es)? Is the post-colonial state's autonomy relative or substantive? Does the state perpetuate a system of domination rather than that by a particular ruling class? Who are these ruling classes who constitute 'the dominant coalition'?

The paper deals with one particular concrete case – that of the post-colonial Indian society to look at the evolving relation of State to class within it. In the process consideration has been given to the extent to which the models of the 'class nature' of the State developed in the context of the post-colonial societies apply to the complex social formations of India.

The most important effort in this direction has been undertaken by Pranab Bardhan.[4] Bardhan argues that the Indian state should be treated as an autonomous actor which has been playing far more important role in the process of shaping and moulding class power than *vice versa*. In the first decade after the political independence, the personnel of the state elite in India enjoyed an independent authority and prestige that made them both the main actors in the process of the socio-economic development of India. This goes without saying that this happened despite the presence of the class constraints. As Bardhan observes, "The state elite that inherited the power at the time of independence enjoyed enormous prestige and a sufficiently unified sense of ideological purpose about the desirability of using state intervention to promote national, economic development, it redirected and restructured the economy and in the process exerted great pressure on the proprietary classes. This led to considerable complexity and fluidity in the composition of the proprietary classes and their relationship with the State."[5] However Bardhan concedes that over the period, with the strengthening of the main proprietary classes (the industrial and agrarian bourgeoisies), the autonomous behaviour of the state has been confined more and more to its 'regulatory' rather than its 'developmental' functions.[6]

Doing a factual study of the political economy of Indian state, Bardhan has discussed the nature of the industrial bourgeoisie (as a whole). Answering as to why this class should be considered as a dominant proprietary class and as the principal beneficiary of the state policies.[7] Bardhan argues that the industrial bourgeoisie led by the top business houses has, "supported the Government policy of encouraging import substituting industrialization, quantitative trade restrictions providing automatically protected domestic markets, and of running a large public sector providing capital goods, intermediate products and infrastructural facilities for private industry, often at artificially low prices."

He goes on to add that the Indian state, since mid-fifties, "has created several public lending institutions loans from which form the predominant source of private industrial finance – an elaborate scheme of industrial and import licences has been allowed to be turned to the advantage of the industrial and commercial interests. they were designed to control. The richer industrialists having better 'connections' and better access have got away with the lion's share in the bureaucratic allocations of the licences thus pre-empting capacity creation and sheltering oligopolistic profits."[8] Thus though the small scale industrial sectors has also flourished since independence, it has been the big houses who have benefitted most from the economic policies implemented by the Indian state over the years.[9]

Agrarian bourgeoisie, the second proprietary class in the Bardhan's dominant coalition, has been helped by the land reforms measures undertaken by the post-colonial Indian state. The measures of this class has also benefitted immensely from the state's agricultural policies providing financial and technical aids to them.[10] Bardhan points out that the fact that the agrarian bourgeoisie is numerically greater in number than the industrial bourgeoisie has also gone in the favour of the former. Taking the size of landholdings as a criterion[11] for the classification, Bardhan observes that roughly nineteen per cent of the rural agricultural population can be considered as belonging to the agrarian bourgeoisie.[12]

The 'professionals', is the third dominant proprietary class in the Bardhan's dominant coalition. Bardhan has mainly focused over the professionals of the public bureaucracy and the public sector white-collar workers. Pranab Bardhan characterise the professionals as a new class of rentiers.[13] To substantiate his stand, Bardhan argues that along with physical assets, possession of certain kinds of knowledge and skill *i.e.* administrative, managerial, scientific and technical should also be considered as private property which has taken different forms. To put it in Bardhan's words, "If physical capital can be the basis of class stratification, so can be human capital in the form of education, skills and technical skills expertise."[14] Bardhan goes on to argue that because of their privileged positions and accessibility to different state organs, these professionals manage to "direct education investments away from the masses (they) have been able to protect their scarcity rent, and by acquiring licence giving powers at various levels of bureaucracy some of them have increased their capacity to multiply this rental income."[15]

While making an argument for the 'professionals' to be treated as a part of the 'dominant coalition', Bardhan focuses entirely on the professionals of the public bureaucracy endorsing the nation of 'cultural capital/human capital', introduced by Pranab Bardhan, Ashok Rudra[16] has recently come out with the concept of 'Intelligentsia' as the third class in the dominant coalition. Rudra also endorses Bardhan's argument that in India one finds a dominant coalition comprising of the industrial and agrarian bourgeoisie. Rudra's 'intelligentsia' is very much an extension of Bardhan's third proprietary class *i.e.* the 'professionals'. Intelligentsia as a social category includes the professionals both from inside and outside the bureaucracy.[17] In fact Rudra's approach, as Andre Beteille argues, clears the way for the inclusion of even public sector workers in the third 'ruling class' namely the intelligentsia.[18] Going back to Rudra, he argues that the 'intelligentsia' as a class does not produce. However it gets a share in the surplus appropriated and disposed of by the other two proprietary classes *i.e.* the industrial and agrarian bourgeoisies. This becomes possible for the intelligentsia because it plays a vital role in sustaining exploitative class rule. So whereas the industrial and the agrarian bourgeoisies are the partners in the ruling coalition primarily due to their non-vacillating commitment to preserving exploitative system, the intelligentsia is there simply because of its vacillating/flexible class interests. As such the said class has no inflexible interest in the preservation of the exploitative capitalist system in India. Thus the fact that the intelligentsia being a vacillating class which in part or whole can any time swing to the side of revolution, enables the class to emerge out not only one of the partner in the ruling coalition but also the leader of the ruling classes.[19]

Sudipta Kaviraj,[20] while making an effort to write a narrative of the Indian politics in terms of actual political actors, in addition to its structural analysis has characterised the nature of the class basis of Indian state as coalitional in nature. Kaviraj argues that a dominant coalition of the industrial bourgeoisie, rich peasantry and a state elite of professionals impose structural constraints on policy choices and their implementation. Apart from the industrial bourgeoisie, Kaviraj mentions rich peasantry as the dominant social class which has benefitted immensely from the 'slow disingenous and uneven legal transformation' that took place under the garb of the land reform measures. Describing the role of the 'Professional groups' (more so its political and bureaucratic segment) as 'functionally' crucial[21] to the dominant coalition, Kaviraj goes on to spell out the reasons. To quote him at length, "Coalitional Politics ... requires political mediation which is often provided by intellectual groups which are the major mediators between the state and the people, they perform an increasingly large role in the state sector after the bureaucratic translation of the concept of development and must be, in purely economic terms, one of the largest unequal beneficiaries of social transforamtion."[22] The professionals, especially their political and bureaucratic segments control over state resources which gives them the allocative power of the resources among the constituent classes of the dominant coalition. Thus whereas the power of the other dominant classes, *i.e.* rich peasantry and the bourgeoisie emanate from their control over processes of production, the strength of the professional groups as a class arise out of their strategic control over the allocation of the resources. Kaviraj goes on to argue that the state officials in India are quite competent in taking up the policy decisions which may go contrary to the incumbents of the dominant coalition. It happens primarily because the Indian state provides a terrain for contestation among and between the ruling classes. It is in these interstices of class conflict that Kaviraj locates the relative autonomy of the post-colonial state in India.[23]

Sanjeeb Mukherjee,[24] another relative autonomist, has also characterised Indian politics as a coalitional politics in class sense. The heterogeneous character of Indian bourgeoisie, lack of consciousness on the part of this bourgeoisie to visualise its own class interests and its desire to have political stability in the country are the factors which, according to Mukherjee, necessitate the presence of an autonomous state in India. Moreover as the indigenous bourgeoisie shares the political power with the other dominant classes *i.e.* the feudal landed peasantry, capitalist agrarian bourgeoisie and the metropolitan bourgeoisie. As Mukherjee puts it, "the dominant classes could be identified as the big bourgeoisie and medium, regional bourgeoisie, the metropolitan (foreign) bourgeoisie and their Indian agents, both comprador capitalists and comprador managerial bourgeoisie, the bureaucratic and professional elite, the capitalist landlords and rich peasants, and the semi-feudal landlords and ex-princes. These, headed by the big bourgeoisie, constitute the power bloc holding state power."[25]

Prabhat Patnaik, Amiya Kumar Bagchi, C.P. Bhambri, Susheela Kaushik, Gailomvedt, Goran Therborn, Monoranjan Mohanty and Achin Vanaik are among the Marxist social scientists who have insisted that a dominant coalition of the ruling classes have operated to impose structural constraints on policy choices and implementation in the autonomous Indian state.

With reference to above Prabhat Patnaik[26] argues that state power in India continues to be based on a coalition between the bourgeoisie post-colonial and the large landowners. Thus the relatively autonomous state in India has, "to maintain the balance of the class coalition (by effectively curbing any constituent group that became too strong)."[27] Pertinently in one of his writings Patnaik has favoured the inclusion of the professionals and bureaucrats as members of the ruling classes in India.[28] The same view has been presented in a well built form in the arguments of Amiya Kumar Bagchi.[29] C.P. Bhambri another Marxist academic too treats Indian state as relatively autonomous in nature which manages, "the conflicting and competing social interests of the bloc of ruling classes."[30] Bhambri also attributes Indian state with "the authoritarian tendencies in meeting the economic crises and their manifestations in social and political crises."[31] Susheela Kaushik does not treat Indian state as a 'total agent of the bourgeois class (es)'. According to her the post-colonial Indian state does retain a certain autonomy which it pursues in certain circumstances. Citing K. Marx, she treats India as a relatively backward country where the classes have not developed fully and in this transitional state there is a mixture of the feudal and the bourgeois classes. Caste and tradition further complicate the mode of operation. In fact her views are very nearer to the position of Charles Bettleheim who holds the opinion that while the industries in India are moving more and more towards a capitalist mode of production, the agricultural scene continues to be feudal or semi-feudal.[32] Thus in this 'Paradoxical situation prevailing in Indian state, Susheela Kaushik finds the expression of class contradictions or conflicts – "conflicts among the big business houses, between the big business on the one hand and smaller capital on the other, between the industrial capitalists and the emergent Kulaks or agricultural capitalists, between the rich farmers and landlords, and between the national bourgeoisie and regional bourgeoisie."[33] These class conflicts result in making the ruling coalition fragmented.[34] Susheela Kaushik goes on to single out the big business as the strongest element of the ruling coalition[35] but at the same time she cautions that the Indian state is not to "be identified with any one fragment of the ruling class."[36] Though Goran Therborn refers to a single industrial class with its fractions and not to a ruling coalition of industrial and agrarian bourgeoisie, his observation is not without relevance here. He says that the capitalist relations of production tend to create an internally competing peacefully disunited ruling class.[37] The 'peaceable disunity' referred in the context of the relationship between the agrarian and industrial bourgeoisie, Therborn goes on to argue that the development of capitalism has stimulated the expansion of petty commodity production, before tending to destroy it. As a result, he says that the commercialization of agriculture transformed a self subsistent peasantry into an agrarian petty bourgeoisie with interests of its own.

Thus in India, according to Therborn, a sizeable agrarian bourgeoisie hegemonizing a significant part of an even larger rural petty bourgeois layer has emerged as a partner in the ruling class alliance. Gail Omvedt has aptly highlighted the economic weight of this class in the dominant class coalition. A rural capitalist farming family thus, today may have some children in the services, own small shops or businesses. "After independence, rich peasants, landlords, and the emerging capitalist farmers began to invest on wider scale, rather than simply consuming surplus. The establishment of tiny transport companies, tea shops, small flour mills, brick kilns, were all part of this process. Some moved into trade in direct competition with previous merchant classes/castes. With the establishment of co-operative sugar factories the new kulaks fought the domination of urban industrialists and merchants and in the process transformed some of their wealth into accumulation in India's second biggest industry. The spread of rural education with the establishment of numerous societies running schools and colleges has also been largely their work."[38] Thus the social and political weight of the rich peasantry *vis-a-vis* the industrial bourgeoisie has grown. A view endorsed by Kandadi Seshadri who observes that "Dominant rural landlord element has taken its position at the state and local levels (and) is able to bargain for more and more from the nation. It raises the cry for price-hike for agricultural commodities coupled with subsidisation of inputs, converts agriculture into capitalist methods, co-opts the men from the bureaucracy and political parties, flouts the land legislations and using caste and other such primordial loyalties builds up support."[39]

Coming back to the issue of the ruling class alliance, Manoranjan Mohanty, a Marxist political scientist, has also mentioned about the existence of a ruling class combination comprising of the feudal, semi-feudal, capitalist and also neo-capitalists. Mohanty opines that the concrete situation in the Indian state demands that this ruling class combination operates in a multitude social network of domination which in turn makes the Indian state relatively autonomous. He puts it as follows, the ruling classes in India, "have internal contradictions and additionally there are the contradictions of class, caste, nationality etc. This objective situation allows the state agencies to enjoy a degree of autonomy."[40] These contradictions have resulted in the duality of the state process in India. To quote his hypothesis, "Reality of the liberal democratic process combined with authoritarian trends, promotion of capitalist economy and controls over it, centralization of state authority and the steady growth of regional forces, an increasingly coercive state apparatus and administration of programmes of a welfare state, an emerging techno-managerial system pursuing non-secular policies, and at the international level being independent and dependent at the same time are some of the indications of this duality."[41] The duality is due to the existence of pre-capitalist forces which continue to function in the post-colonial period making the social formations complex in nature. Making his hypothesis clear Mohanty argues that the liberation struggles against the colonial power generated forces of democratic action in society. The same forces also challenged the traditional inequitous order. The democratization in the post-colonial state has been constrained by complex social and ideological forces. This factor leads to the duality of the Indian state. Mohanty puts it as follows, "Due to the historical process in India which led to a complex social formation having elements of both pre-capitalism and capitalism, class, caste and ethnicity, the process of capitalist development in India has acquired a duality or has contradictory trends.[42] Mohanty finds these trends being manifested in practically all spheres of the state processes in India. As for the presence of the authoritarian trends present in Indian state process, Dipankar Gupta also opines that the Indian state is not hegemonic. He argues that Indian state is repressive. While examining the issue regarding the relevance of the theory of relative autonomy of State in the context of India, Dipankar Gupta argues that it is not 'relative autonomy', but it is 'relative anarchy' that makes the post-colonial Indian State take this or that function.[43]

The paper has concentrated on the recent Marxist analysis of the dominant class relationships in the relatively autonomous Indian state. As has been evident, there has been a widespread agreement that the two dominant classes of the Indian social formation are the agrarian bourgeoisie and the industrial bourgeoisie. However, beyond this, the autonomy of the Indian state has posed serious problems and considerable disagreement on what social class/groups constitute in full the ruling oligarchy, power bloc, ruling-class alliances, dominant coalition/ruling coalition and therefore, on how to characterize the Indian state in the adequate manner. In fact the relative autonomy enjoyed by the post-colonial Indian state has compelled the Marxists to raise the issue of the 'professionals', 'intelligentsia', 'the state bureaucracy' or the 'middle classes'.[44] This is because as Rehman Sobhan points out, "indigenous trading bourgeoisie, and/or owning capital in industry had developed along with a class of Government officials, professionals associated with trade, the judicial system, education and public services."[45] These professionals or a class of Government officials who pursue many policies which do not meet with the approval or support of the industrial or agrarian bourgeoisies. Thus as Ashwanik Ray points out, political power in India, "has been exercised by various coalitions of the heterogeneous elite of the country, drawn from its multiple social plurality based on ascriptive identities including the bourgeoisie and other Marxist social groups". He goes on to argue that "the professional middle class has played a significant role in the power structure of the political system since its inception."[46]

To reiterate, in the post-colonial societies, including India, where the indigenous bourgeoisie is relatively well developed the state has to be seen as, Theda Skocpol has argued in 'Organization' and 'realistic' tenus.[47] The Indian state, in fact acts as an organization with certain interests which are distinct from those of the dominant classes. This has been possible because, as Hamza Alavi has rightly pointed out overdeveloped post-colonial state mediates between "the competing interests of three propertied classes, namely the metropolitan bourgeoisie, the indigenous bourgeoisie and the landed classes, while at the same time acting on behalf of them all to preserve the social order in which their interests are embedded, namely the institutions of private property and the capitalist mode as the dominant mode of production."[48] In the context of the presence of the metropolitan bourgeoisie, one may agree with Achin Vanaik[49] who concedes that the indirect hold and influence of foreign capital/imperialism remains powerful and inescapable." However, as Bharat Patankar and Gail Omvedt[50] have pointed out, the indigenous bourgeoisie may be in alliance with metropolitan capital but it qualifies in its own right as a ruling class in the dominant coalition. In a recent study A. Mukherjee and M. Mukherjee reach on a similar conclusion about the autonomy of the Indian economy and the irrelevance of metropolitan bourgeoisie as a social force in the basic class relationships of the Indian social formation.[51] This remains true even in the wake of the recent economic crisis confronting the Indian state.

References

1. Martin Carnoy, 'The State and Political Theory', Princeton, Princeton University Press, 1983, p. 3.
2. Peter Evans, A. Rueschemeyer and Thedor Skocpol (eds.), 'Bringing the State Back In', Cambridge, Cambridge University Press, 1985.
3. The debate was initiated by Hamza Alavi. Hamza Alavi, 'State in the Post-Colonial Societies' in Harry Goulborne (ed.), 'Politics and State in The Third World', London, Macmillan, 1979.
4. Pranab Bardhan, 'The Political Economy of Development in India', Oxford, Oxford University Press, 1984.

5. *Ibid.*, p. 38.
6. *Ibid.*, pp. 38-39.
7. A.R. Desai, however, is not so much influenced by the capacity of the bourgeoisie. Exploring the relationship between the state and the capitalist class in India, he comes to the conclusion that, "the history of the practices of the capitalist class attempting to industrialize the economy clearly reveals that it has not been able to do so, nor will it be able to pursue such a path... The Indian experience clearly indicates (the) incapacity of the national bourgeoisie." A.R. Desai, India's Path of Development: A Marxist Approach, Bombay, Popular Pvt., 1984, p. 87.
8. *Ibid.*, p. 40-41.
9. As Mathew Kurien has pointed out, "The Dynamics of Public Sector in India has worked in the direction of strengthening capitalism under the ageis of the monopoly capital. In the name of socialist pattern the system which has in fact been created is state capitalism wherein the 'Public Sector' or the 'State Sector' operates as a necessary vehicle for profit maximization by the private capitalists and for expanding the share of the capitalist class particularly monopoly capital, in the national income." Mathew Kurien, 'Class Character of Indian State' in Mathew Kurien (ed.) 'India — State and Society', Madras, Orient Longmans, 1975, p. 95.
10. K. Seshadri, "Marxism and Indian Polity', New Delhi, People's Publishing House. 1988, Ch. VII.
11. Pranab Bardhan's cut off to decide the rich farmer category is roughly ten acres. Lloyd J. Rudolph and Susane H. Rudolph make fifteen acres their cut off point thereby expanding the size of the 'bullock capitalists'. It is this social category which, according to them is the new ruling class in India. L.J. and S.H. Rudolph, 'In Pursuit of Lakshmi: The Political Economy of the Indian State', Bombay, Orient Longman, 1988.
12. Gail Omvedt, who has made an attempt to trace the caste-class nexus in modern rural India, believes that about fifteen per cent of all rural families came under the rich farmer category and these include capitalist farmers, capitalist landlords, and a minority of feudal landlords. Refer: Gail Omvedt, 'Class, Caste and Land in India', in Gail Omvedt (ed.), 'Land, Caste and Politics in Indian States', Delhi, Authors Guild, 1982.
13. For similar views, Refer: K.N. Raj 'The Politics and Economics of Intermediate Regimes'. Cited in H. Srikanth, 'Nature of Indian State: Reflections on Dominant Marxist Interpretations of Indian State', Teaching Politics, Vol. XIV, No. 1, 1988, p. 45.
14. Pranab Bardhan, N. 4, p. 51.
15. *Ibid.*, p. 52-53.
16. Ashok Rudra, 'Emergence of the Intelligentsia as a Ruling Class in India', Economic and Political Weekly, 21 June 1989.
17. In one of his recent article, Pranab Bardhan has clarified that he refers to the same social category as does Ashok Rudra in his treatment of the professionals as a dominant class. Thus Bardhan concedes that the members of the 'Professionals' can come from both inside as well as outside the bureaucracy. However Bardhan is uneasy with the term Intelligentsia. Refer : Pranab Bardhan, 'The Dominant Class', Economic and Political Weekly, 21 January 1989, p. 155.
18. Refer: Andre Beteille, 'Are the intelligentsia a ruling class?', Economic and Political Weekly, 21 January 1989, Ashok Rudra, N. 16.

19. Ashok Rudra, N. 16.
20. Sudipta Kaviraj, 'Indira Gandhi and Indian Politics', Economic and Political Weekly, 20 September, 1986.
21. However, Kaviraj unlike Ashok Rudra does not treat the professionals (including the intellectuals) as the dominant partner in the dominant coalition, *Ibid.*, p. 1697.
22. *Ibid.*, p. 1697.
23. *Ibid.*, p. 1698.
24. Sanjeeb Mukherjee, 'Class Struggles and the State in India', in Zoya Hasan, S.N. Jha and Rasheedudin Khan (eds.), 'The State, Political Processes and Identity: Reflections on Modern India', New Delhi, Sage Publication, 1989.
25. *Ibid.*, p. 99.
26. Prabhat Patnaik, 'Imperialism and Growth of Indian Capitalism' In K. Mathew Kurien (ed.) 'India-State and Society: A Marxist Approach', N. 9.
27. *Ibid.*, p. 149.
28. Prabhat Patnaik, 'Imperialism and Growth of Indian Captialism' in Robin Blackborn (ed.), 'Explosion in Subcontinent', London, Pelican, 1985, p. 52.
29. Amiya Kumar Bagchi, 'Political Economy of Underdevelopment', Cambridge, Cambridge University Press, 1982, p. 179.
30. C.P. Bhambri, 'The Indian State: Conflicts and Contradictions' in Zoya Hasan, S.N. Jha and Rasheedudin Khan (ed.), 'The State, Political Processes and Identity: Reflections on Modern India', N. 24, p. 85.
31. *Ibid.*, p. 85.
32. Charles Bettleheim, 'India Independent', London, George McGee, 1968.
33. Susheela Kaushik, 'Nature of the Indian State', Teaching Politics, February 1988, p. 58.
34. Susheela Kaushik, 'Elections in India: Its Social Basis', New Delhi, K.P. Bagchi and Company, 1982, p. 27.
35. Susheela Kaushik, N. 33, p. 60.
36. *Ibid.*, p. 59.
37. Goran Therborn, 'The Role of Capital and the Rise of Democracy', New Left Review, 103, May-June, 1977.
38. Gail Omvedt, 'Capitalist Agriculture and Rural Classes in India', Bulletin for Concerned Asian Scholars, July-August, 1983, p. 43.
39. K. Seshadri, 'Marxism and Indian Polity', N. 10, p. 227-228.
40. Manoranjan Mohanty, 'The Contemporary State', Teaching Politics, February, 1988, p. 50-51.
41. Manoranjan Mohanty, 'Duality of the State Process in India', In Ghanshyam Shah (ed.) 'Capitalist Development: Critical Essays' Bombay, Popular Prakashan, 1990, p. 151.
42. *Ibid.*, p. 160.
43. Dipankar Gupta, 'Anarchy and Capitalism', Seminar, 367, March, 1990.
44. One early expression of this can be found in the speculation on how applicable to India was Kalecki's concept of the 'Intermediate Regime'. In this regime, the ruling classes are namely the lower middle class and the rich peasantry. They organized an appropriate arrangement with the upper middle class. The state was the

dynamic entrepreneur and state capitalism served the interests of the lower middle class. Refer: M. Kalecki, 'Social and Economic Aspects of Intermediate Regimes' in his 'Socialism and the Mixed Economy: Selected Essays', Oxford, Oxford University Press, 1972.

45. Rehman Sobhan, 'The State and Development of Capitalism: The Third World Perspective', in Krishna Bhardwaj and Sudipta Kaviraj, eds. "Perspectives on Capitalism: Marx, Keynes, Schumpeter and Weber', New Delhi, Sage Publications, 1990, p. 249.
46. Ashwani K. Ray, 'Towards the Concept of a Post-Colonial Democracy: A Schematic View' in Zoya Hasan, S.N. Jha and Rasheeduddin Khan (ed.) 'The State, Political Processes and Identity: Reflections on Modern India', N. 39, p. 138.
47. Theda Skocpol, 'State and Revolution: Old Regimes and Revolutionary Crisis' in Theory and Society, January-March, 1979.
48. Hamza Alavi, 'State in the Post-Colonial Societies', in Harry Goulbourne, 'Politics and State in the Third World', N. 3, p. 42.
49. Achin Vanaik, 'The Painful Transition: Bourgeois Democracy in India', London, Verso, p. 12.
50. Bharat Patankar and Gail Omvedt, 'The Bourgeois State in Post-Colonial Formations', The Insurgent Sociologist, 9 (Spring), 1980. pp. 23-38.
51. A. Mukherjee and M. Mukherjee, 'Imperialism and Growth of Indian Capitalism in the Twentieth Century', Economic and Political Weekly, 12 March, 1988.

CHAPTER V

INDIAN 'LEFT': VIEWS ON STATE AND SOCIETY

The Traditional Communist Parties have approached the nature of the class character of the Post-colonial Indian State from varying perspectives and with reference to differing specific theoretical issues. These involve the nature and composition of the ruling classes the specific relation of the local bourgeoisie to the western bourgeoisie, and of each to the State. The present chapter attempts to analyse these divergent characterisations of the growing trends in the class relations in India as has been perceived by the Traditional Communist Parties – the CPI, the CPI (M) and the CPI (M.L.). Pertinently these theoretical debates about the class character of Indian State provided the bases of the divergent strategic and tactical formulations of the Indian Communists.

With reference to above it would be apt to note that the divergent interpretations with regard to the class character of the post-colonial Indian State are not to be attributed to the break up of the United Communist Party of India. Even during the period of unity within the Communist Party, diversity of opinion remained. This became sharply evident as despite the acceptance of the 1951 Programme, Statement of Policy and Tactical line, the diversity of opinion with regard to its interpretation remained among the Indian Communists. The 1951 documents passed at all India Party Conference held at Calcutta characterised the post-colonial Indian State as a semi-Colonial and Semi-feudal state. Identifying imperialism and feudalism as the main enemy of the Indian masses, the tactical line asked for the 'replacement of the present state upholding the imperialist feudal order by a people's democratic state'. In fact there was no basic departure from the assessment made in the 1948 political thesis of the Calcutta Congress as in 1951 statement of policy maintained that the Nehru Government mainly served "the interests of feudal landlords and big monopoly financiers and behind them all, the vested interest of British Imperialism." However, the perspective of an immediate advance to a socialist

revolution by intertwinning the tasks of the democratic revolution and the socialist revolution was given up. Instead, the 1951 programme called for the setting up of a 'people's democracy created on the basis of a coalition of all democratic anti-feudal and anti-imperialist forces in the country.' Moreover the tactical line dismissed the possibility of a 'fundamental transformation in the country by parliamentary methods.' To quote the CPI statement of Policy of 1951, "There are a large number of people who think that this Government can be replaced by a People's democratic Government by utilizing the parliament ushered in by the new Constitution ... Even a liberal would now feel ashamed to maintain, let alone the Communist party and other democrats and revolutionaries that this Government and the classes that keep it in power will ever allow us to carry out a fundamental democratic transformation in the country by parliamentary methods alone. Hence the road that will lead us to freedom and peace, land and bread, as outlined in the programme of our party, has to be found elsewhere." Later the statement mentioned at one place: "All action of the masses in defence of their interest to achieve liberation is sacrosanct. But one action history does not sanction and that is individual terrorism. Individual terrorism is directed against individuals of a class or system and is carried out by individuals or groups and squads." The condemnation of the individual terrorism was to dissociate the CPI from the tactics advocated by the former General Secretary, B.T. Ranadive. From their discussions with the Soviet Communist leaders, the Indian communists felt that the course of the future revolution in India would not blindly follow either the Russian path or the Chinese path. On the one hand the presence of an organised working class seemed to enable India to go for the revolutionary tactics used by the Russian Bolshevics, then on the other hand, the preponderance of the poor and landless peasants in India made Indian Communists to take up Maoist line seriously.

In such a concrete situation, the CPI spelt out in detail about its tactics in a secret document known in Party circles as the 1951 Tactical Line. The document contended that the complete liquidation of feudalism, the distribution of all land held by feudal owners among the peasants and agricultural workers, and achievement of full national independence and freedom "could not be realized in a peaceful way but was possible 'through an armed revolution' of the people." Referring to the need for guerilla warfare in the countryside, the document held that, "Partisan war must be one of the major weapons in our armoury... it has to be combined with other major weapons – that of strike and uprising in the cities led by the armed detachment of the working class .... It is absolutely essential to combine two basic factors – the partisan war of the peasants and workers' uprising in the cities. (Adding that the) onslaught of the enemy against the partisan forces against liberated areas will have to be hampered and paralysed by Mass Strike Actions." Pertinently the secret documents were never circulated among the party ranks but were later publicised by the Maoists to show how the CPI leadership persisted in violating the line after that.

Thus these documents had seeds of all the three lines that grew up later in the Indian Communist movement as the statement of policy reflected an uneasy compromise between the Rightists and Leftists in the United CPI. This was one of the reason as to why the 1951 tactical line was abandoned. Reasonably good performance of the CPI in the first general election aroused hope among the Communists about the parliamentary means for grabbing political power. In its foreign policy also, the independent foreign policy followed by Indian State raised question mark about its 'semi-colonial' nature. Consequently the CPI welcomed "the role played by the Indian Government on a number of important international issues in the recent period, a role appreciated by the peace-loving masses and states" in its Congress held in Madurai in 1953. The trend continued when the CPI met for its fourth Congress at Palghat in 1956. The party report stated that "despite vacillations and inconsistencies that still persist to some extent, it (India's foreign policy) is essentially an independent policy". Meanwhile the Communist Party of erstwhile Soviet Union (CPSU) had also sanctioned for Parliamentarism and non-violent means to change a bourgeois Government. This paved the way for the CPI to give up the 1951 characterization of the Indian State as a semi-colonial state. Taking the line of CPSU, the CPI conceded that Indian state had achieved political independence despite its economic dependence over the western Imperialism. Indian State was consequently characterised as 'Landlord bourgeois state in which the bourgeoisie is the leading force.' Thus the CPI took a soft and flabby attitude towards class conflicts and had the conciliatory attitude towards the ruling party or the landed peasantry which supported it by the middle of the fifties. Taking a distinct turn towards right, the Palghat Congress of the CPI in 1956 passed a resolution saying, "The struggle to build the democratic front involves a policy of simultaneous unity with and struggle against the bourgeoisie ... It should not be conceded that the democratic front will be an anti-Congress front ... Although the political party of the bourgeoisie which has taken many landlords in its folds, the Congress has among its members a vast number of democratic elements. It has an anti-imperialist and democratic elements. It has an anti-imperialist and democratic tradition." Quite obviously the Palghat Congress as well as the Amritsar Congress in 1958 indicated the upper hand of the rightists inside the united CPI. However the Leftists under the leadership of P. Sundarayya, Basavapunniah and Hanumantha Rao – all from Andhra and who were to break away eventually from the CPI and form the CPI (M) – submitted a note at the Palghat Congress. They reiterated in their note that Indian state remained 'semi-colonial and dependent' and that the then Indian Government was 'collaborating with British Imperialism.'

The lack of homogeneity among the members of the United communist Party continued unabated throughout the fifties and the beginning of the sixties. The Crunch came in 1962 due to the war between China and India. The impact of the division of the international Communist movement also broadened the division. Consequently the formal split came in 1964 and the United Communist Party got divided into the CPI and the CPI (Marxist). The CPI continued to be dominated by the rightists whereas the CPI(M) members comprised of the Leftists, formerly part of the United C.P.I.

The CPI has been characterising the state in India as the organ of the class rule of the national bourgeoisie as a whole, in which the big bourgeoisie and landlords, led by the big bourgeoisie, who are increasingly landlords. This interpretation adopted by the Eighth Congress of the CPI and reiterated in successive party Congresses, has a number of important implications. First among others is that the ruling class in post-colonial Indian State is the national bourgeoisie as a whole. This national bourgeoisie includes both the big bourgeoisie with or without links with the western imperialist powers. The second implication is that the feudal landlords despite having strong links with the power structure does not pass as one of the dominant ruling classes. Third implication is that though the CPI recognises the powerful influence of the big bourgeoisie yet this class is not considered as having dominant position in the ruling structure. Fourth and the last implication is that the powerful influence of the big bourgeoisie and the national bourgeoisie's links with the landlords are supposed to give rise to the reactionary pools in the state power, although otherwise state power is by implication anti-imperialist, anti-feudal and progressive in nature. Hence the CPI's political line is geared towards the programme of national democratic revolution, according to which the national bourgeoisie should be supported to carry out the democratic revolution. Within this framework, the CPI supports what it calls the progressive policies of the national bourgeoisie. The CPI points at the Government policies like nationalisation of banks and industries, development of public sector, anti-monopoly measures, anti-colonial measures, etc. to support its claim. Similarly the non-aligned foreign policy of the Indian state has been always hailed by the CPI as the anti-imperialist and pro-socialist content. On the Agrarian front, the CPI sees a clear trend of capitalist development, which was facilitated by the abolition of Zamindari and Land Reforms measures and accentuated by the green revolution. The political process of elections and Panchayati Raj, according to the CPI, has induced this process in a more significant manner. Thus the CPI's belief in progressive character of national bourgeoisie make them give a call for 'National Democratic Front' which remains directed against feudalism, imperialism and monopolies. They seek to set up a 'national democracy' as against the 'People's democracy' of the CPI and the CPI (ML). 'National Democracy' is to be achieved by this national democratic front engaged in mass agitations and mobilising public support for winning a majority in the parliament. Their programme of National Democratic Revolution through peaceful means follows the completion of the preceding stage of the anti-imperialist and anti-feudal revolution which the national bourgeoisie is at present trying to accomplish. Thus the national bourgeoisie will be an ally in the effort to bring national democratic revolution. In this context the CPI's orientation is different from the programme of people's democratic revolution of the CPI(M) and the CPI (ML).

The CPI(M) programme adopted at the Calcutta Congress provided a different ideological assessment about the character of Indian State. It described Indian State as "the organ of the class rule of the bourgeoisie and landlords, led by the big bourgeoisie, who are increasingly collaborating with foreign finance capital in pursuit of the capitalist path of development". This formulation has been reiterated consistently. The above formulation has a number of important implications. First implication is that the ruling class is composed of two constituent classes, *i.e.* the big bourgeoisie and the landlord. Second implication is that of these two constituent classes, the dominant position is held by the big bourgeoisie and that over the years this trend has grown further. Third and the last implication is that the big bourgeoisie is collaborating with foreign finance capital for furthering capitalist development.

The CPI(M) contends that the stage of the general national united front, joined by different classes, was completed in 1947 when Indian achieved independence. However, the Indian bourgeoisie had gradually assumed leadership of the national liberation movement and thus in the post-colonial phase it captured the state. Afterward in order to strengthen its position, it collaborated with western imperialism and also with feudal and semi-feudal elements in India. Consequently they have also pointed out India's excessive dependence on foreign economic assistance and the poor performance on the Agrarian reforms. They also point towards the big bourgeoisie amassing riches at the cost of the medium and small scale sectors. To overcome this state of affair, CPI(M) firmly believes that the stage of the democratic revolution is essentially anti-feudal, anti-imperialist, anti-monopoly and democratic. Almost reiterating the Principles of Mao stated in his 'On New Democracy', the CPI (M) programme says, "it is not the old type bourgeoisie led democratic revolution, but a new type of People's democratic revolution, organised and led under the hegemony of the working class." Their programme, therefore, seeks to establish a People's democratic front consisting of the working class as leading class in firm alliance with peasants, revolutionary intelligentsia and the national bourgeoisie whose vacillating character they should be cautious about. This formulation of the CPI(M) very much replicate the Maoist notion of the United Front.

The CPI(ML) has not remained a homogenous party divided and redivided into several factions or groups. However even now, almost all the M-L groups in spite of many tactical differences, still hold on to the view that India is a semi-feudal and semi-colonial state, which has not even gained independence. Hence the CPI (ML) programme of 1970 described State power in India as being in the hands of 'Feudalism, compradore-bureaucrat, capitalism, imperialism and social imperialism.' Thus they drew a parallel with the Chinese revolution. It would be pertinent to quote People's Daily: "India under Congress rule is only nominally independent, in fact it is nothing more than a semi-colonial and semi-feudal country. The Congress Administration represents the interests of the Indian feudal princes, big landlords and bureaucrat compradore capitalists. Internally, it oppresses the Indian people without any mercy and sucks their blood, while internationally it serves its new boss, U.S. imperialism and its number one accomplice, the Soviet revisionist ruling clique, in addition to its old suzerain British Imperialism, thus selling out the national interests of India in a big way. So imperialism, Soviet revisionism, feudalism and bureaucrat compradore capitalism weigh like big mountains on the backs of the Indian people, first of all the toiling masses of workers and peasants. This formulation about the class composition of the Indian ruling class has several important aspects. First of all is the fact that bureaucrat compradore capitalists as well as the big landlords are the ruling classes in India. Secondly, these classes are nominally independent and are entirely dependent upon the imperialist master of the Indian ruling classes is the United States – Soviet Union no longer exists. Third and the last aspect is that the CPI(ML) under Charu Mazumdar's leadership formulated its view essentially in terms of the 'three big mountains' which Mao had originally identified as dominating and exploiting China: Imperialism, Feudalism and Compradore-bureaucrats.

Thus the CPI (ML) programme adopted by its party Congress in 1970 declared, "The basic task of the Indian revolution is to overthrow the rule of feudalism, compradore-bureaucrat capitalism, imperialism and social imperialism." Correspondingly the CPI(ML) identified four major contradictions : "contradiction between imperialism and social imperialism on the one hand and our people on the other, between feudalism and the broad masses of the people, between capital and labour and the contradiction within the 'ruling classes'." Out of them 'the contradiction between the landlords and the peasantry, *i.e.* the contradiction between feudalism and the broad masses of the Indian people is the principal contradiction in the present phase.'

With reference to above, the viewpoints of the CPI(ML) can be compared with the CPI(M)'s view. The CPI (ML) did not accept that India was a fully independent state while the CPI(M) thought it was, but it remained under the influence of foreign monopoly capital. Furthermore, the CPI(ML) considered the landlords as the main enemy while to the CPI(M) the big bourgeoisie was the leading force in state power though 'The task of carrying out radical agrarian reforms was the first and foremost.'

In order to fight the class enemies, the CPI(ML) chalks out their strategy in the following manner: "The working class fully relies on the landless and poor peasants and firmly united with the middle peasants and even wins over a section of the rich peasants while neutralising the rest." As far as the urban components of the United Front were concerned, the CPI(ML) declared the 'Urban Petty bourgeoisie and revolutionary intellectuals as reliable allies in the revolution' but did not clearly formulate their line towards the national bourgeoisie. Having dismissed the Indian bourgeoisie as essentially compradore in nature, they spoke only about 'the small and middle bourgeoisie, businessmen and bourgeoisie intellectuals as 'vacillating and unstable allies of the democratic revolution.' Just as Mao spoke of the dual character of the national bourgeoisie the CPI(ML) has also pointed towards the dual role of these classes. Their programme, however, did not suggest any concrete method of winning over this class. This is in contrast to the view of the CPI(M) which contends that the national bourgeoisie would be compelled to join the 'People's democratic front' when foreign monopolists and big bourgeoisie strengthen their hold at their further expense. The CPI (ML) approach to the united front can be summed up with the help of the following statement: "This front, however, can only be built up when worker-peasant unity is achieved in the course of armed struggle and after red political power is established at least in some parts of the country."

In course of the last two decades the Naxalite groups have confronted the question of characterising the Indian State in the light of several debates on the nature of the Indian bourgeoisie, the extent of development of capitalism in agriculture the linkage with foreign powers and so on. Some of the new thinking as these issues is reflected in the formulations of the CPI(ML) groups in the eightees. The CPI (ML) led by Vinod Mishra which is linked with the Indian People's Front (IPF) characterises its enemy, for example, as 'feudal remnants, compradore bureaucrat capital and imperialism.' In other words despite defining Indian State as semi-feudal, they now admit the significant development of capitalism in Indian agriculture. They also admit that Indian State is politically independent, but remains economically dependent. Because of the deep penetration of Finance capital into Indian society it continues to be semi-colonial. In their programme finalised at their Party Congress in January 1988, they say that "the big bourgeoisie in alliance with the landlords lead the Indian State". Pertinently it comes close to the CPI(M) formulation except for the reference to the compradore-bureaucratic capital.

Like China's People's democratic revolution, the CPI(ML) regards agrarian revolution as the axis and the Principal contradiction at this state is also defined by them as the one between feudalism and the broad masses of the people. In parallel with the Chinese revolution, the CPI(ML) groups in India regard the working class as the leader of the revolution and the peasantry as the main revolutionary force. The Chinese revolution had been carried out by four class united front with worker-peasant alliance as its core. Almost the same line has been accepted by the CPI(ML) groups. The Vinod Mishra group's programme for instance, says that it "relies on poor peasant and rural proletariat, resolutely unites with the middle peasant and even wins over a section of the capitalist farmer while neutralising the rest ... small and medium size capitalists and bourgeois intellectuals are vacillating and unstable allies of the democratic revolution."

The CPI-ML (People's War Group) or the P.W.G. has more or less continued the 1970 characterisation of the Indian State. Pertinently, they do not grant much credence to the development of capitalism in India. This is contrary to the view of Vinod Mishra group. The CPI-ML (Chandra Pulla Reddy Group) stands inbetween them. In practice all the three leading M-L groups have been studying the tribal question and the caste question involving the issue of the contradiction between tribal peasants and landlords, and between the rich peasants and agricultural labourers belonging to the scheduled castes.

Thus there has been serious differences among these three traditional Communist parties *i.e.* the CPI, the CPI(M) and the CPI (ML) regarding the class composition of the Indian ruling class. In fact the character of the Indian bourgeoisie remain a debatable issue among the Communist parties especially in the context of the simultaneous existence of dependence and independence represented by India's big bourgeoisie. The nature of the contemporary world economy and the policies of the Indian state allow this duality to flourish in the Indian capitalism. Moreover the growing influence of the middle class as an expanding sector and playing a critical role in the State process in India has not acquired much attention among the Communist parties either. The concrete fact that the class contradiction is intertwined with the caste contradiction also requires fresh thinking among the traditional Communist parties. In fact the interpretations of the traditional Communist parties with regard to the nature of Indian state are mostly economistic and instrumentalist in their content. Thus the 'Indian State' has been characterised as 'Landlord bourgeoisie State' or 'semi-feudal/semi-colonial State because of the presence of the certain semi-feudal and colonial hangovers in the economy and culture. However, the relative autonomy of the Indian State and the specificity of politics has been completely ignored by the Indian Communist parties who retain their mechanical understanding of the Indian State based on the Marxian classics and their subjective study of it.

References

Muzaffar Ahmed, *Communist Party of India: Years of Formation*, Calcutta, National Book Agency, 1969.

Sumanta Banerjee, *India's Simmering Revolution*, London, Zed Books Ltd., 1989.

Paul Brass and Marcus F. Franda eds., *Radical Politics in South Asia*, Massacheusetts: The MIT Press, 1973.

Bipan Chandra ed., *The Indian Left: Critical Appraisals*, New Delhi, Vikas, 1983.

Biplab Das Gupta, *Class Character of the Ruling Class in India* in K. Mathew Kurian (ed) *India—State and Society: A Marxian Approach*, Bombay, Orient Longman, 1975.

Sobhan Lal Das Gupta, *Comintern, India and the Colonial Question*, Calcutta, K.P. Bagchi, 1980.

Sohail Jawaid, *The Naxalite Movement in India*, New Delhi: Associated Publishing House, 1980.

P.C. Joshi, *Congress and the Communists*, Bombay, PPH, 1944.

Narhari Kaviraj, *October Revolution and National Liberation*, Calcutta, K.P. Bagchi, 1978.

Sudipta Kaviraj, *The Split in the Communist Movement in India*, Unpublished Ph.D. Dissertation, Jawahar Lal Nehru University, 1979.

Susheela Kaushik, *Elections in India, Its Social Basis*, Calcutta, K.P. Bagchi and Company, 1982.

Manoranjan Mohanty, *Maoist Revolutionary Strategy: A Reinterpretation*, The Institute for Defence Studies and Analysis Journal, Vol. II, No. 3, January, 1970.

——, *The Political Philosophy of Mao Tse Tung*, New Delhi, Macmillan, 1978.

——, *Ideology and Strategy of the Communist Movement in India*, Thomas Pantham and Kenneth L. Deutsch (eds.), Political Thoughts in Modern India New Delhi, Sage, 1986.

——, *Chinese Revolution and the Indian Communist Movement* Unpublished Seminar Paper presented in International Conference on 'New Perspectives on the Chinese Revolution', International Institute of Social History, Amsterdam, 8-13, January, 1990).

E.M.S. Namboodiripad, *Kerala—Yesterday. Today and Tomorrow*, Calcutta, National Book Agency Pvt. Ltd., 1968).

——, *The Communist Party in India (Marxist)*, Journal of Constitutional and Parliamentary Studies, Vol. V, No. 4, Dec. 1971.

T.J. Nossiter, *Communism in Kerala*, Delhi: Oxford University Press, 1982.

Gail Omvedt, *The Left in India*, Journal of Contemporary Asia, Vol. 15, No. 2, 1985.

G.D. Overstreet and Marshall Windmiller, *Communism in India*, Bombay: Perennial Press, 1960.

Mohan Ram, *Indian Communism — Split within a split*, Delhi: Vikas, 1969.

——, '*The Communist Movement in India*' in Kathleen Gough and Hari P. Sharma (eds.), *Imperialism and Revolution in South Asia*, New York, M.R. Press, 1973.

Bhabani Sen Gupta, '*Communism in Indian Politics*', New York, Columbia University Press, 1972.

P. Sundarayya, *Telangana People's Struggle and It's Lessons*, Calcutta, CPI(M) Publication, 1972.

Sadanand Talwar, *Under the Banyan Tree: The Communist Movement in India*, New Delhi, Allied, 1985.

Myron Weiner, *The Party Politics in India*, New Jersey, Princeton University Press, 1957.

SELECTED BIBLIOGRAPHY

Alavi, Hamza, "Character of State in Pakistan", in *Studies in Indo-Pak* Relations, edited by V.D. Chopra, New Delhi: Patriot, 1984.

—, "Class and State", in *Pakistan: The Roots of Dictatorship*, edited by H. Gardezi and J. Rashid, London: Zed Press, 1983.

—, "The State in Post-Colonial Societies: Pakistan and Bangladesh", in *Imperialism and Revolution in South Asia*, edited by Kathleen Gough and Hari Sharma, New York: Monthly Review Press, 1973.

Ahmed, Muzaffar, *Communist Party of India: Years of Formation*, Calcutta: NBA, 1969.

Amin Samir, *Unequal Development: An Essay on the Social Formations of Peripheral Capitalism*, New York, Monthly Review Press, 1976.

Anderson, Perry, *Lineages of the Absolutist State*, London, New Left Books, 1974.

Avineri, Shlomo, (ed.), *Karl Marx on Colonialism and Modernization*, New York, Doubleday, 1968.

Bagchi, Amiya K., *Political Economy of Underdevelopment*, Cambridge, Cambridge University Press, 1982.

Banerjee, Diptendra, *Marxian Theory and the Third World*, New Delhi, Sage Publications, 1985.

Banerjee, Sumanta, *India's Simmering Revolution*, London, Zed Books, 1984.

Bardhan, Pranab, *The Political Economy of Development in India*, Oxford, Basil Blackwell, 1984.

Beteille, Andre. "Are the Intelligentsia a Ruling Class?" *Economic and Political Weekly*, January 21, 1989.

Brass, Paul and Marcus F. Franda, *Radical Politics in South Asia*, Massacheusetts, MIT Press, 1973.

Carnoy, Martin, *The State and Political Theory*, Princeton, N.J., Princeton University Press, 1984.

Chandhoke, Neera, "Expanding the Marxian Notion of the Post-

Colonial State", *Social Scientist*, Vol. 19, Nos. 9-10 (October-November), 1991.

Chandra, Bipan, *The Indian Left: Critical Appraisals*, New Delhi, Vikas, 1983.

Davis, Horance, "Capital and Imperialism: A Landmark in Marxist Theory", *Monthly Review*, September, 1967.

Das Gupta, Sobhan Lal, *Comintern, India and the Colonial Question*, Calcutta, K.P. Bagchi, 1980.

Draper, Hal, *Karl Marx's Theory of Revolution*, Vol. I, State and Bureaucracy, New York, Monthly Review Press, 1977.

Desai, A.R., *India's Path of Development: A Marxist Approach*.

Evans, Peter A., Rueschemeyer and Theodor Skocpol, *Bringing the State Back In*, Cambridge, Cambridge University Press, 1985.

Frank, A.G., *Crisis in the Third World*, London, Heinemann Educational Books Ltd., 1981.

Ghosh, Suniti K., "Marx on India", *Monthly Review*, January, 1984.

Gupta, Dipankar, "Anarchy and Capitalism", *Seminar*, 367, March, 1990.

Hamilton, Nora, *The Units of State Autonomy: Post-revolutionary Mexico*, Princeton, N.J., Princeton University Press, 1982.

Higgot, Richard, *Political Development Theory*, New York, Croom Helms, 1983.

Hobsbawm, E.J. (ed.), *Karl Marx: Pre-capitalist Economic Formations*, London, Lawrence and Wishart, 1964.

Jawaid, Sohail, *The Naxalite Movement in India*, New Delhi, Associated Publishing House, 1980.

Jessop, Bob, *The Capitalist State*, Oxford, Martin Robertson, 1982.

King, Roger, *The State in Modern Society*, London, Macmillan, 1980.

Kasfir, Nelson, ed., *State and Class in Africa*, London, Frankcass, 1984.

Kaushik, Susheela, *Elections in India: Its Social Basis*, Calcutta, K.P. Bagchi, 1982.

—, "Nature of the Indian State". *Teaching Politics*, February, 1988.

Kaviraj, Narhari, *October Revolution and National Liberation*, Calcutta, K.P. Bagchi, 1978.

Kaviraj, Sudipta: "Indira Gandhi and Indian Politics", *Economic and Political Weekly*, September 20, 1986.

Kaviraj, Sudipta, "Marxian Theory and Analysis of Indian Politics" in *A Survey of Research in Political Science*, Vol. 4, New Delhi, Allied Publishers, 1984.

Kurien, Mathew, ed., *India–State and Society*, Madras: Orient Longmans, 1975.

Lefebvre, Henry, *The Sociology of Marx*, London: Allen Lane, The Penguin Press, 1968.

Miliband, Ralph. "Marx and the State" *Socialist Register*, edited by Ralph Miliband and John Savillee, London, Merlin Press, 1965.

—, *Marxism and Politics*, London, Oxford University Press, 1977.

Mohanty, Manoranjan, "Ideology and Strategy of the Communist Movement in India". In *Political Thoughts in Modern India*, edited by Thomas Pantham and Kenneth L. Deutsch, New Delhi, Sage, 1986.

Mohanty, Manoranjan, *The Political Philosophy of Mao Tse-Tung*, New Delhi, Macmillan, 1978.

Namboodiripad, E.M.S., "The Communist Party in India (Marxist)", *Journal of Constitutional and Parliamentary Studies*, Vol. V, No. 4, December, 1971.

Omvedt, Gail. "The Left in India", *Journal of Contemporary Asia*, Vol. 15, No. 2, 1985.

Overstreet, G.D. and Marshall Windmiller, *Communism in India*, Bombay, Perennial Press, 1960.

Patankar, Bharat and Gail Omvedt, "Bourgeois State in Post-Colonial Social Formations". *Economic and Political Weekly*, December, 1977.

Patnaik, Prabhat, "Imperialism and Growth of Indian Capitalism" in *Explosion in Subcontinent*, edited by Robin Blackburn, London, Pelican, 1975.

Poulantzas, Nicos, *Political Power and Social Classes*, London, New Left Books, 1975.

Rudolph, L.I. and S.H. Rudolph, In *Pursuit of Lakshmi: The Political Economy of the Indian State*, University of Chicago Press, 1987.

Rudra, Ashok, "Emergence of the intelligentsia as a Ruling Class in India", *Economic and Political Weekly*, June 21, 1989.

Sainz, Perez. "Towards a conceptualization of State Capitalism in the Periphery", *The Insurgent Sociologist*, 9 (Spring), 1980.

Samoff, Joel, "Class, Class Conflict and the State in Africa", *Political Science Quarterly*, 27 (Spring), 1982.

Shivji, Issa, *Class Struggles in Tanzania*, London, Heinemann, 1976.

Sklar, Richard, "The Nature of Class Domination in Africa", *The Journal of Modern African Studies*, 17(4), 1979.

Sobhan, Rehman, "The State and Development of Capitalism: The Third World Perspective" in *Perspectives on Capitalism: Marx, Keynes, Schumpeter and Weber*, edited by Krishna Bhardwaj and Sudipta Kaviraj, New Delhi, Sage Publications, 1990.

Swainson, N. "The Rise of a National Bourgeoisie in Kenya", *Review of African Political Economy*, 8 (January-April), 1977.

Therborn, Goran, "The Role of Capital and the Rise of Democracy", *New Left Review*, 103 (May-June), 1977.

Thorner, Daniel, "Marx on India and the Asiatic Mode of Production", *Contributions to Indian Sociology*, Vol. 6, 1964.

Vanaik, Achin, *The Painful Transition: Bourgeois Democracy in India*, London, Verso, 1990.

Von Freyhold, Michelae, "The Post-Colonial State and its Tanzanian Version", *Review of African Political Economy*, 8 (January-April), 1977.

Ziemann and Lanzendorfor, "The State in Peripheral Societies" in *Socialist Register* edited by Ralph Miliband and John Saville, London, Merlin Press, 1977.

INDEX

INDEX

F

G

H

I

J

K

L

M

N

O

P